The Uninsured

Other Books in the Current Controversies Series

Drug Legalization

Factory Farming

Forensic Technology

The Green Movement

Medical Ethics

Nuclear Energy

Oil

Teen Pregnancy and Parenting

Vegetarianism

Current
CONTROVERSIES

The Uninsured

Debra A. Miller, Book Editor

GREENHAVEN PRESS
A part of Gale, Cengage Learning

GALE
CENGAGE Learning™

Detroit • New York • San Francisco • New Haven, Conn • Waterville, Maine • London

Christine Nasso, *Publisher*
Elizabeth Des Chenes, *Managing Editor*

© 2011 Greenhaven Press, a part of Gale, Cengage Learning

For more information, contact:
Greenhaven Press
27500 Drake Rd.
Farmington Hills, MI 48331-3535
Or you can visit our Internet site at gale.cengage.com

Articles in Greenhaven Press anthologies are often edited for length to meet page requirements. In addition, original titles of these works are changed to clearly present the main thesis and to explicitly indicate the author's opinion. Every effort is made to ensure that Greenhaven Press accurately reflects the original intent of the authors. Every effort has been made to trace the owners of copyrighted material.

Cover image © Ed Kashi / Corbis.

LIBRARY OF CONGRESS CATALOGING-IN-PUBLICATION DATA

The uninsured / Debra A. Miller, book editor.
        p. cm. -- (Current controversies)
    Includes bibliographical references and index.
    ISBN 978-0-7377-5638-8 (hardcover) -- ISBN 978-0-7377-5639-5 (pbk.)
    1. Medically uninsured persons--United States. 2. Medical care--United States. I. Miller, Debra A.
    RA413.7.U53U535 2011
    362.1'0425--dc22

                                                                    2010051680

Printed in the United States of America
1 2 3 4 5 6 7 15 14 13 12 11

Contents

Foreword   15

Introduction   17

Chapter 1: Is the Lack of Health Insurance a Serious Problem in America?

Chapter Preface   22

Yes: The Lack of Health Insurance Is a Serious Problem in America

Children Who Lack Health Insurance Are   25
More Likely to Die in Hospitals

Karen Pallarito

A study by the Johns Hopkins Children's Center found
that children without health insurance were 60 percent
more likely to die in the hospital than children who had
insurance. Overall, the study found that an estimated
seventeen thousand children in the United States may
have died during the last twenty years because they didn't
have health insurance.

The Lack of Adequate Health Insurance Is a   28
Leading Cause of Bankruptcies in America

ConsumerAffairs.com

A nationwide survey of bankruptcy filers showed that
more than 60 percent of personal bankruptcies in the
United States in 2007 were caused by health care costs
associated with a major illness. This finding means there
has been a 50 percent increase in the number of bankruptcies caused by medical expenses since a similar study
in 2001.

The Recession Is Increasing the Number   31
of Uninsured

Nayla Kazzi

The majority of Americans still rely on employer-provided health care insurance, but the recession has caused the loss of hundreds of thousands of jobs each month. The Center for American Progress estimates that this loss of jobs has caused 2.4 million workers to lose their health insurance, adding to the 46 million of uninsured Americans.

No: The Lack of Health Insurance Is Not a Serious Problem in America

People Without Health Insurance   35
Are Not More Likely to Die
    Megan McArdle

Many commentators cite the link between the lack of health insurance and the risk of death, but the studies supporting this claim are based on relatively old data and do not completely control for factors that may cause the uninsured to have more health risks than the rest of the population. Also, other studies support the opposite conclusion—that the uninsured do not have a higher risk of death than insured people.

Most of the Uninsured Are Young, Healthy,   42
and Financially Well-Off
    Michael D. Tanner

The number of uninsured is driving the health care debate but the reality is that most of the uninsured are young, in good health, and 43 percent have annual incomes higher than $55,125. In addition, a quarter of the uninsured are eligible for government-paid health programs and another 10 million uninsured are immigrants, including approximately 5.6 illegal immigrants—categories that should not be counted in the numbers of uninsured Americans.

The Majority of Voters Say Cost,   45
Not Lack of Coverage, Is the Biggest
Health Care Problem
    Rasmussen Reports

A March 2010 national telephone survey found that 54 percent of Americans polled think cost is the biggest problem with health care, while only 24 percent say the lack of universal coverage is the main problem. Eleven percent cite the quality of care as their concern, 2 percent note scheduling problems, and 10 percent are undecided.

Chapter 2: Does Access to Health Insurance Improve People's Health?

Chapter Preface   49

Yes: Access to Health Insurance Improves People's Health

Health Insurance Is Important to the Health   52
and Well-Being of Both Children and Adults
Institute of Medicine
Research clearly shows that both children and adults benefit greatly from health insurance. Children with health insurance are more likely to have a stable source of medical care; to get immunizations, prescriptions, asthma care, and dental services; and have fewer hospitalizations and sick days. Adults without insurance are more likely to delay or forgo doctor's visits, be diagnosed with late-stage cancers, suffer poorer health outcomes, experience a lower quality of life, and die from acute medical conditions.

Insurance Coverage Is Strongly Related   58
to Better Health Outcomes
Jill Bernstein, Deborah Chollet, and Stephanie Peterson
Health insurance coverage improves health outcomes for consumers by reducing health care costs; helping people secure preventive care, prescription drugs, mental health treatment, and other services; and improving continuity of health care. Insurance coverage also improves the nation's social and economic strength by preventing developmental problems in children, increasing workforce productivity, decreasing hospitalizations, and reducing the costs of government programs.

Not Having Health Insurance Increases   65
the Risk of Cancer Death

Walter Jessen

The lack of adequate health insurance coverage correlates
with reduced access to care and poorer outcomes for
cancer patients. Uninsured people are less likely to be
screened for cancer, more likely to be diagnosed at an
advanced disease stage, and more likely to die from their
cancers than insured patients.

**No: Access to Health Insurance Does Not
Improve People's Health**

Health Insurance and More Medical Care   69
Do Not Necessarily Produce Health Benefits

Maggie Mahar

The studies linking the lack of insurance to death are inconclusive. The uninsured may not receive proper management of chronic diseases, but they do receive emergency room treatment once they are seriously ill. The
real reason behind most premature deaths is poverty and
related factors such as social issues, personal behaviors,
and environment.

The Lack of Health Care Is Not Responsible   76
for Low US Life Expectancy

Ronald Bailey

Low life expectancy in the United States is often cited as
a sign that the nation's health insurance system is failing,
but studies show that America provides good care for
many diseases and medical conditions. It is more likely
that bad health habits of Americans, such as smoking
and obesity, are the reason for low longevity rankings.

High Deductibles and Benefit Limits Can   79
Diminish Health Care Coverage, Even for
the Insured

Drew Altman

The focus of the health care debate has been on large premium hikes by health insurance companies, but families often mitigate these premium increases by agreeing to higher deductibles and limits on benefits. After many years of this pattern, even insured people end up with insurance that pays only about half of their health care bills.

Expanded Access to Health   83
Insurance Is Not the Only Tool
to Improve Population Health
Harold Pollack

Studies have reached opposite results concerning whether health insurance is linked to mortality; health insurance probably does save lives, and universal health insurance no doubt makes people healthier. However, there are more cost-effective ways to improve health and save lives—for example, by increasing cigarette taxes, preventing the spread of infectious diseases, providing reproductive health services, devoting funds to substance abuse prevention and treatment, and reducing child poverty.

Chapter 3: Should the Purchase of Health Insurance Be Mandated by the Government?

Overview: How the Individual Mandate in   90
the 2010 Health Reform Law Will Work
Alec MacGillis

The Patient Protection and Affordable Care Act—health reforms enacted in 2010—requires all citizens and legal immigrants to have health insurance, either through their employers or by purchasing plans through new state-based insurance exchanges. Those who fail to comply with this individual mandate must pay a fine. However, there will be legal challenges and resistance to the mandate, and no one knows whether it will succeed.

Yes: The Purchase of Health Insurance Should Be Mandated by the Government

Americans Should Support the Individual   97
Insurance Mandate Because It Is Necessary
to Make Health Reform Work
Jonathan Cohn

Requiring everyone to have health insurance—called the individual mandate—is a feature of health care systems throughout the world and is necessary to make health reform work in the United States. In order to require insurance companies to cover everyone, including people with preexisting medical conditions, it is necessary to enlarge the insured population to also include healthy people. Otherwise, people could game the system by waiting until they are sick before buying insurance.

The Individual Insurance Mandate in   101
Health Reform Is Not Unprecedented
in American History
Maggie Mahar

Some commentators argue that requiring people to buy health insurance is unprecedented and that the government has never required people to buy any good or service. This is not true; the Militia Act of 1792 required every able-bodied white male citizen to enroll in his state's militia and arm himself with a gun and other equipment to defend the country. The problem of uninsured Americans threatens our economy and our society just as much as an attack from abroad.

An Individual Insurance Requirement in   107
Health Reform Will Be Constitutional
Erwin Chemerinsky

Health care reform opponents argue that the individual mandate is unconstitutional, but they are wrong. Congress is clearly authorized to require people to purchase health insurance or pay a fine under its power to regulate commerce among the states. Congress also could justify this as an exercise of its taxing and spending power since it is similar to Social Security taxes, which everyone is required to pay.

**No: The Purchase of Health Insurance Should
Not Be Mandated by the Government**

The Individual Insurance Mandate in   111
Health Reform Is Bad Public Policy
Jon Walker

The individual mandate is neither good politics nor good policy. If progressives want to create universal health insurance in the most cost-effective way, there are other policy solutions that are better. The most ideal solution is a universal single-payer health care system, similar to Medicare, along with other options.

There Are No Precedents for the Individual   114
Insurance Mandate in the New Health
Reform Law

Julia Shaw

The second Militia Act of 1792 is not a precedent for creating an individual health insurance mandate, not only because the act only applies to a narrow subset of society, but also because the act is founded on a solid constitutional basis—the power of Congress to organize a militia. Also, the Commerce Clause does not support the mandate because it does not authorize requiring individuals to purchase a specific service.

The Supreme Court Is Likely to Find the   118
Individual Insurance Mandate
Unconstitutional

Randy Barnett

Supporters of health reform quickly dismissed constitutional challenges to the law's individual insurance mandate, claiming that it is justified under the Commerce Clause of the US Constitution. However, the law's defenders have shifted their constitutional theories and are now claiming constitutional authority under Congress's power to tax. This switch is too late, since the Supreme Court will not consider the penalty enforcing the mandate to be a tax because Congress did not call it or treat it as a tax in the legislation.

Chapter 4: Will the PPACA Improve Medical Care for the Uninsured?

Chapter Preface   124

Yes: The Patient Protection and Affordable Care Act (PPACA) Will Improve Medical Care for the Uninsured

The Health Care Reform Law Creates   **128**
Tremendous Opportunities to Improve the
Quality of US Health Care

Mark B. McClellan

The new health care reform legislation will give millions
of Americans access to health care, but it also includes
provisions designed to improve the quality of health
care. For example, the law will collect information on the
quality and cost of care, improve payment systems to
avoid paying quantity of care rather than quality, and
create pilot and demonstration projects to test other reform ideas.

Uninsured Women Will Benefit Greatly   **131**
from the PPACA's Reforms

*Sara R. Collins, Sheila Rustgi, and Michelle M.
Doty*

Women have always faced higher health care costs than
men and are just as likely to be uninsured. The Patient
Protection and Affordable Care Act (PPACA) will insure
up to 15 million women who are now uninsured, reduce
women's health care costs, and provide improved coverage due to various insurance industry reforms.

Health Insurance for the Uninsured Will   **136**
Improve Care for All Americans

Eric B. Larson

Providing universal access to health insurance is important for all Americans, because the high number of uninsured Americans even has negative effects on people with
good health insurance. For example, medical providers
have shifted from providing valuable basic health care to
providing more profitable procedures and tests, making
it harder for everyone to access quality health care.

No: The Patient Protection and Affordable Care
Act (PPACA) Will Not Improve Medical Care for
the Uninsured

Health Care Reform Expands Coverage   **139**
in the Wrong Way, by Sacrificing Quality
of Care

Kathryn Nix

The new health care reform law will not help the uninsured for a variety of reasons. The law will leave 23 million Americans without coverage; expand coverage largely by expanding eligibility for Medicaid—a reform that will result in less choice and lower quality of coverage; and impose new insurance regulations that will cause insurance premiums to skyrocket.

The PPACA Will Not Remedy Access and   145
Quality Problems in Cancer Care
John Geyman

Health care reform is unlikely to remedy many of the systemic problems facing cancer patients. At least 23 million people will still be uninsured or underinsured; the costs of cancer care will continue to rise; and health insurance will only become more unaffordable. In addition, choice of coverage will be limited for some people, and the new reforms will not prevent insurers from gaming the new system to maximize profits.

The History of Health Coverage Expansion   151
Shows That It Leads to Runaway Costs
Peter Suderman

Even before passage of the Patient Protection and Affordable Care Act (PPACA), various states have enacted health care reforms, but each time they ended up being more expensive than projected. The Congressional Budget Office has said that the PPACA would lead to a reduction in the national deficit, but these projections are uncertain, and the PPACA could wreck the federal budget.

Health Care Reform Is a Disaster   155
for All Americans
Peter Ferrara

Obamacare will be disastrous for US health care. It is a federal government takeover of health care that will increase health costs for families, businesses, and government; cut Medicare payment rates for doctors and hospitals by 30 percent; and impose new taxes on Americans.

Organizations to Contact   164

Bibliography   169

Index   174

Foreword

By definition, controversies are "discussions of questions in which opposing opinions clash" (Webster's Twentieth Century Dictionary Unabridged). Few would deny that controversies are a pervasive part of the human condition and exist on virtually every level of human enterprise. Controversies transpire between individuals and among groups, within nations and between nations. Controversies supply the grist necessary for progress by providing challenges and challengers to the status quo. They also create atmospheres where strife and warfare can flourish. A world without controversies would be a peaceful world; but it also would be, by and large, static and prosaic.

The Series' Purpose

The purpose of the Current Controversies series is to explore many of the social, political, and economic controversies dominating the national and international scenes today. Titles selected for inclusion in the series are highly focused and specific. For example, from the larger category of criminal justice, Current Controversies deals with specific topics such as police brutality, gun control, white collar crime, and others. The debates in Current Controversies also are presented in a useful, timeless fashion. Articles and book excerpts included in each title are selected if they contribute valuable, long-range ideas to the overall debate. And wherever possible, current information is enhanced with historical documents and other relevant materials. Thus, while individual titles are current in focus, every effort is made to ensure that they will not become quickly outdated. Books in the Current Controversies series will remain important resources for librarians, teachers, and students for many years.

In addition to keeping the titles focused and specific, great care is taken in the editorial format of each book in the series.

Book introductions and chapter prefaces are offered to provide background material for readers. Chapters are organized around several key questions that are answered with diverse opinions representing all points on the political spectrum. Materials in each chapter include opinions in which authors clearly disagree as well as alternative opinions in which authors may agree on a broader issue but disagree on the possible solutions. In this way, the content of each volume in Current Controversies mirrors the mosaic of opinions encountered in society. Readers will quickly realize that there are many viable answers to these complex issues. By questioning each author's conclusions, students and casual readers can begin to develop the critical thinking skills so important to evaluating opinionated material.

Current Controversies is also ideal for controlled research. Each anthology in the series is composed of primary sources taken from a wide gamut of informational categories including periodicals, newspapers, books, US and foreign government documents, and the publications of private and public organizations. Readers will find factual support for reports, debates, and research papers covering all areas of important issues. In addition, an annotated table of contents, an index, a book and periodical bibliography, and a list of organizations to contact are included in each book to expedite further research.

Perhaps more than ever before in history, people are confronted with diverse and contradictory information. During the Persian Gulf War, for example, the public was not only treated to minute-to-minute coverage of the war, it was also inundated with critiques of the coverage and countless analyses of the factors motivating US involvement. Being able to sort through the plethora of opinions accompanying today's major issues, and to draw one's own conclusions, can be a complicated and frustrating struggle. It is the editors' hope that Current Controversies will help readers with this struggle.

Introduction

"Researchers comparing the health care systems of developed countries have consistently ranked the United States last or next to last on issues such as quality, efficiency, and effectiveness of care."

Some commentators have called the US health care system the envy of the world, praising its cutting-edge medical technologies, with an emphasis on new drug research and state-of-the-art medical facilities. Yet researchers comparing the health care systems of developed countries have consistently ranked the United States last or next to last on issues such as quality, efficiency, and effectiveness of care. Studies have found, for example, that even though the United States spends more than any other country on health care, it has the highest rates of infant mortality and the lowest levels of life expectancy of almost any other developed nation. One of the problems with US health care, according to many health experts, is the high number of uninsured—that is, people without any type of health insurance coverage. In fact, according to the US Census Bureau, 46.3 million Americans, or about 15 percent of the total population, had no health insurance in 2008.

Unlike the United States, most other developed nations have created health insurance systems that offer affordable insurance coverage that covers almost everyone, typically under some type of government-regulated or government-run program. In the United States, however, only the elderly, the disabled, and the very poor are covered by US government health programs such as Medicare and Medicaid. The majority of other Americans get their health insurance through their employers in a privately operated system. This system leaves the unemployed, the self-employed, and many near-poor people to buy their own insurance in the individual private insurance market—often a very expensive option because of high premiums, large yearly deductibles, and costly co-pays for each visit to the doctor. In fact, some people in America cannot buy health insurance at any price, because they have preexisting medical conditions or illnesses that insurers say would make such coverage unprofitable. Furthermore, even Americans who have insurance, either through their employers or policies that they have purchased on their own, can find themselves underinsured in the event of a serious illness or trauma. This is typically because most health insurance policies in the United States only pay for about 80 percent of medical costs, with both a yearly and a lifetime per-person cap on the amount the insurer will pay—restrictions that shift a significant portion of health costs to consumers and force many Americans into medical bankruptcies.

The reason the US health care system differs so dramatically from that of other developed countries stems largely from the unique way that health insurance developed in America. The idea of health insurance took root in the United States during the Great Depression—a severe and worldwide economic downturn that occurred in the 1930s—when people found themselves unable to afford the rising costs of medical care. Around this time, a system of private, nonprofit insurance was created to cover large groups of employees. One of the first efforts to provide prepaid health care, for example, was initiated by Baylor Hospital in Dallas, Texas, in 1929. It provided up to twenty days of hospital care for local teachers who paid a monthly premium of about fifty cents. This idea spread around the country to other hospitals and eventually evolved into a national Blue Cross system that covered not only hospital stays, but other types of health care. The early Blue Cross insurers charged everyone the same premium regardless of age, sex, or preexisting conditions—a system called community rate—and premiums were kept low, supported by government tax deductions. It was a system based on a simple principle—that if a large enough pool of people was created to spread the risk, the healthy could subsidize the sick so that each person was taken care of when they were in need of health care. The Blue Cross system established a tradition of private sector health insurance in the United States.

In the 1940s, World War II helped to create America's system of employer-based health insurance. The war produced a tight labor market at home because so many workers were in active duty with the armed forces. When the government imposed wage controls on employers as part of the war policies, many employers began offering health insurance as an employee benefit to attract qualified workers. The federal government encouraged this trend by offering employers tax deductions for health care expenses and allowing the insurance benefit to be tax free to employees. When World War II ended in 1945, employers continued to offer health insurance because by then it had become a highly popular job benefit, and the employer-based health insurance system expanded to become the US model.

Beginning in the 1950s, however, the nonprofit Blue Cross health insurance plans began to be overtaken by large, for-profit commercial insurance companies like Prudential, Aetna, and Metropolitan Life. Unlike Blue Cross—which charged everyone the same premium based on the community rate system—commercial insurers tried to attract healthy people by offering them cheaper policies that reflected their individual health risks. These companies charged the old and the sick, who had higher individual health risks, much higher rates, sometimes refusing to cover them at all. This strategy—called experience rating—undercut Blue Cross by skimming off the youngest, healthiest consumers. Soon Blue Cross was forced to adopt this same experience-rating model, and the US system of for-profit health insurance was born.

Many health care experts argue that this unique US system of employer-based, private, for-profit health insurance has led to a health care crisis characterized by exploding health care costs and a growing uninsured population without access to adequate medical care. Over the years, many efforts have been made to reform US health care, resulting in some changes. For example, in 1965 the United States adopted the landmark Medicare/Medicaid law that created a government-run program to provide medical care for older Americans, the disabled, and the poor. In 1973, Congress passed the Health Maintenance Organization Act—a law designed to promote managed care health insurance plans that seek to control health care costs by controlling the quantity and quality of health care services provided to beneficiaries. Additionally, in 1997, the United States expanded government aid to poor children through the State Children's Health Insurance Program (SCHIP).

Most recently, in March 2010, President Barack Obama championed historic health care reforms that were passed by Congress as the Patient Protection and Affordable Care Act (PPACA). Although it retains the employer-based, private insurance system, this reform seeks to cover millions of uninsured Americans by requiring insurers to grant coverage to both sick and healthy people and by mandating that everyone must have health insurance, with government subsidies to help those who cannot afford it.

Whether the PPACA will improve health care for those people who are currently uninsured is one issue covered by *Current Controversies: The Uninsured*. The authors of the viewpoints included in this volume also address more fundamental questions such as whether the lack of health insurance is a serious problem, whether access to insurance leads to better health, and whether the government should mandate the purchase of health insurance.

CHAPTER 1

Is the Lack of Health Insurance a Serious Problem in America?

Chapter Preface

Proponents of health reform often cite the number of uninsured as a central problem that must be solved to create an effective US health care system. According to 2009 statistics from the US Census Bureau, 46.3 million Americans, or roughly 15 percent of the total population, have no health insurance. This is a large number, but critics say a careful examination of how this number breaks down reveals some interesting facts.

One striking fact, for example, is that most of the uninsured are not old or desperately poor, largely because the elderly, the poor, and many children are now covered by government health programs such as Medicare, Medicaid, and the State Children's Health Insurance Program (SCHIP). In fact, according to the US Census Bureau, most of the uninsured earn more than $25,000 per year and 20 percent have incomes above $50,000. Some commentators argue that these figures mean that many uninsured people could afford health insurance but voluntarily choose not to buy it. However, others have pointed out that more than 60 percent of the uninsured earn less than 200 percent of the poverty level, which is only about $44,100 per year for a family of four—hardly enough to afford typical health insurance plan premiums, which can easily run above $12,000 annually.

In fact, many of the uninsured may be relatively young and healthy working-class families who do not receive health benefits from their employers and simply cannot afford to self-pay for individual health insurance policies. According to the Census Bureau, for example, nearly all the uninsured are under age sixty-five, and about 40 percent of the uninsured are between eighteen and thirty-four years old. Approximately 35.2 million uninsured are in families, and 10.7 million are single; about 7.3 million are children. Conservative commentator Michael Tanner claims that 86 percent report being in good or excellent health. Notably, most of the non-elderly uninsured—about 82.8 percent—live in families where the head of the household works. However, these workers apparently do not receive employer-based health insurance; in fact, one in five of the uninsured works in a large company (defined as a firm with five hundred or more employees) that does not pay health benefits.

Furthermore, a significant portion of the uninsured are racial and ethnic minorities or noncitizens—typically sectors of the American population that tend to take low-income jobs with no benefits. In 2008, 30.7 percent of Hispanics were uninsured, as were 19.1 percent of African Americans, 17.6 percent of Asians, and 31.7 percent of Native Americans and Alaska Natives, compared to a 10.8 percent uninsurance rate for whites. Also, according to Census Bureau estimates, 33.5 percent of the uninsured are immigrants, with noncitizens making up 18 percent of this immigrant population. The number of illegal immigrants in this group of uninsured is not exactly known, although some commentators have claimed it is about 5.6 million.

Many health experts argue that the lack of health insurance is damaging not only for the uninsured, but also for their families and the larger society. The Institute of Medicine (IOM), an independent health research group of the National Academy of Sciences, has concluded, for example, that people without health insurance experience poorer health, die sooner, and are more likely to go bankrupt as a result of health costs than those who are insured. However, some commentators argue that just because they are uninsured does not mean that people without insurance go without health care. One study, for example, found that the uninsured receive about 40 percent of the amount of health care received by those with insurance. Many of the uninsured are without insurance only for temporary periods, and people without insurance often can get care at free clinics or hospital emergency rooms—which are federally mandated to provide emergency care. The uninsured also do pay out of pocket for some health care. The Kaiser Family Foundation, for example, estimates that those uninsured for at least part of the year receive $84.3 billion in care during the time they are uninsured, $30 billion of which is paid for out of pocket, leaving $54.3 billion uncompensated. Still, most analysts agree that people without health insurance receive significantly less medical care and consume far fewer medical resources than the insured.

Whether America's uninsured population is a serious problem is a critical issue in the health care debate, and it is the topic addressed by the authors of the viewpoints included in this chapter.

Children Who Lack Health Insurance Are More Likely to Die in Hospitals

Karen Pallarito

Karen Pallarito is a reporter for HealthDay, a health news licensing and syndication service.

An estimated 17,000 children in the United States might have died unnecessarily over nearly two decades because they didn't have health insurance, according to a report from researchers at Johns Hopkins Children's Center in Baltimore.

They found that kids who lacked health insurance were 60% more likely to die in the hospital than were kids who had insurance. After adjusting for such differences as race and gender, uninsured kids were still 37.8% more likely to die than kids with insurance coverage.

The Value of Health Insurance

David C. Chang, codirector of the pediatric surgery outcomes research group at Hopkins and a study coauthor, said he could not think of a medical treatment that has such a dramatic impact on health outcomes as health insurance seemingly does.

"This is actually something we as a society . . . can choose to do something about," he said. "It's literally with the stroke of somebody's pen, this could be changed."

The article was published online Oct. 30 in the *Journal of Public Health*.

Karen Pallarito, "17,000 Child Deaths Linked to Lack of Insurance," MedicineNet.com, October 29, 2009. SOURCES: David C. Chang, Ph.D., M.P.H., M.B.A., co-director, Outcomes Research, Department of Surgery, Johns Hopkins School of Medicine, Johns Hopkins Bloomberg School of Public Health, Baltimore; Bruce Lesley, president, First Focus, Washington, D.C.; Oct. 30, 2009, Journal of Public Health, online Copyright © 2009 HealthDay. All rights reserved. Reproduced by permission.

Bruce Lesley, president of First Focus, a bipartisan child and family advocacy group, noted that data from the U.S. Institute of Medicine have shown that people who are uninsured have a higher mortality rate.

Over an 18-year period though 2005 . . . 38,649 children died while hospitalized.

"You knew that it existed, you knew that there were cases [of child deaths related to lack of insurance], but I think this data is pretty shocking and really points to the need for national health reform," Lesley said.

In one of his first acts after taking office in January, President Barack Obama signed legislation reauthorizing the Children's Health Insurance Program (CHIP). The measure also provided funding for states to add several million more children to the rolls though 2013.

"CHIP has really worked and has been very important and insures about 7 million kids in the country," Lesley said. Still, he said, roughly 6.5 million children who are eligible for Medicaid or CHIP remain uninsured—for whatever reason.

Enrollment barriers are part of the problem, explained Lesley, whose organization endorses legislative proposals to move toward a "default enrollment" system. "The presumption should be the kid's enrolled, and let's figure out what program they're in," he said.

The Study

The Johns Hopkins team looked at the relationship between insurance status and kids' mortality to better inform the CHIP debate.

Using records from two large databases, lead author Dr. Fizan Abdullah, Chang and colleagues examined more than 23 million hospitalizations of people younger than 18.

Over an 18-year period though 2005, 117 million children were hospitalized. Nearly 6 million kids were uninsured at the time of admission. In all, 38,649 children died while hospitalized.

Uninsured kids were 1.6 times more likely to die than children who had insurance.

Assuming that the insured and uninsured populations are identical, the difference in risk of mortality was 60%. The authors' actual predicted mortality is lower, however, because factors such as age, race and gender are associated with risks that affect outcomes, Chang explained.

"The 60% is the theoretical difference, and the 37% is the actual difference that you see in real life," he said. "Our extrapolation is based on that more conservative number."

The study includes some data from the period before CHIP was enacted in 1997. Though fewer kids are uninsured today than two decades ago, Chang said, that would not skew the risk of death from lack of insurance.

And though the study does not prove that being uninsured boosts a child's mortality risk, it does suggest a strong association between insurance status and odds of dying.

"I think the message is insurance is a choice we can make as a society, and this is something that we should consider," Chang said.

The Lack of Adequate Health Insurance Is a Leading Cause of Bankruptcies in America

ConsumerAffairs.com

ConsumerAffairs.com is a consumer news and advocacy site founded in 1998 by James R. Hood, a veteran Washington, D.C., journalist and public affairs executive. The site includes consumer news, recall information, and consumer comments.

A new study finds that more than 60% of personal bankruptcies in the United States in 2007 were caused by health care costs associated with a major illness. That's a 50% increase in the number of bankruptcies blamed on medical expenses since a similar study in 2001.

A Broken System

In an article published in the August 2009 issue of the *American Journal of Medicine*, the results of the first-ever national random-sample survey of bankruptcy filers shows that illnesses and medical bills contribute to a large and increasing share of bankruptcies.

"The US health care financing system is broken, and not only for the poor and uninsured," said Harvard Medical School researcher David U. Himmelstein, M.D. "Middle-class families frequently collapse under the strain of a health care system that treats physical wounds, but often inflicts fiscal ones."

Consumer activists who have been pressing for universal health care coverage applauded the study.

"The rising number of medical bankruptcies among the insured tells us that the patchwork, inadequate coverage offered by private health insurance is bad for our economic health," said Sidney Wolfe, M.D., director, Health Research Group at Public Citizen. "We urgently need a single-payer system that covers everyone, regardless of employment or ability to pay. Expanding private insurance and calling it health reform will fail to prevent financial catastrophe for hundreds of thousands of Americans every year."

In 2007, before the current economic downturn, an American family filed for bankruptcy in the aftermath of illness every 90 seconds; three-quarters of them were insured.

"This study provides further evidence that the US health care system is broken," according to James E. Dalen, M.D., M.P.H., University of Arizona College of Medicine, Tucson. "Medical bankruptcy is almost a unique American phenomenon, which does not occur in countries that have national health insurance. These longtime advocates of a single-payer system give us another compelling reason to work toward this goal as a nation."

The study found that in 2007, before the current economic downturn, an American family filed for bankruptcy in the aftermath of illness every 90 seconds; three-quarters of them were insured. Over 60% of all bankruptcies in the United States in 2007 were driven by medical incidents.

Following up on a 2001 study in five states, where medical problems contributed to at least 46.2% of all bankruptcies, researchers from Cambridge Hospital/Harvard Medical School, Harvard Law School and Ohio University surveyed a random national sample of 2,314 bankruptcy filers in 2007, abstracted their court records, and interviewed 1,032 of them. They designated bankruptcies as "medical" based on debtors' stated reasons for filing, income loss due to illness and the magnitude of their medical debts.

Using identical definitions in 2001 and 2007, the share of bankruptcies attributable to medical problems rose by 49.6%. The odds that a bankruptcy had a medical cause were 2.38 fold higher in 2007 than in 2001.

Many Are Underinsured

According to the study, a number of circumstances propelled many middle-class, insured Americans into bankruptcy. For 92% of the medically bankrupt, high medical bills directly contributed to their bankruptcy. Many families with continuous coverage found themselves underinsured, responsible for thousands of dollars in out-of-pocket costs.

Out-of-pocket medical costs averaged $17,943 for all medically bankrupt families: $26,971 for uninsured patients; $17,749 for those with private insurance at the outset; $14,633 for those with Medicaid; $12,021 for those with Medicare; and $6,545 for those with VA [Veterans Affairs]/military coverage. For patients who initially had private coverage but lost it, the family's out-of-pocket expenses averaged $22,568.

Because almost all insurance is linked to employment, a medical event can trigger loss of coverage. Nationally, a quarter of firms cancel coverage immediately when an employee suffers a disabling illness; another quarter does so within a year. Income loss due to illness was also common, but nearly always coupled with high medical bills.

The Recession Is Increasing the Number of Uninsured

Nayla Kazzi

Nayla Kazzi is a research assistant who focuses on economic policy at the Center for American Progress, a progressive think tank.

The fear of losing your job is a familiar feeling to many Americans today. And for the nearly six-in-ten Americans—59.3 percent—receiving health care through their employer, that fear is often exacerbated by the anxiety that losing a job also means loss of health care coverage—not just for the worker, but often for their family as well.

Employer-Based Health Care

While the share of workers relying on employment-based health care coverage has declined from its peak of 64.2 percent in 2000, access to adequate affordable health care for a majority of Americans is still contingent on their employment status.

Employers are shedding hundreds of thousands of jobs every month—just last month [April 2009] employment declined by 663,000—and the number of uninsured Americans continues to rise.

Sixty-two percent of the American public believes that the current economic turmoil makes it more important than ever to take on health care reform, and the need for comprehensive reform becomes all the more evident as conditions in the economy continue to deteriorate and more Americans become uninsured.

Nayla Kazzi, "More Americans Are Losing Health Insurance Every Day," Center for American Progress, May 4, 2009. Reprinted by permission.

Estimating the Rise in the Number of Uninsured

Forty-six million Americans lacked health care coverage in 2007, when the national employment level peaked and before the current economic recession officially began. Today, that number is markedly higher as many workers who have lost their jobs have also lost their employer-provided health insurance.

Access to adequate affordable health care for a majority of Americans is still contingent on their employment status.

Employers have shed 5.1 million jobs in the last 15 months. Three industries alone—manufacturing, construction, and professional and business services—account for nearly three-quarters of total jobs lost. Manufacturing has shed 1.5 million jobs—1.1 million in durable goods, 367,000 in nondurable goods manufacturing—construction has eliminated 1.1 million jobs; and professional and business services have cut 1.2 million positions.

We estimate that 2.4 million workers have lost the health coverage their jobs provided since the start of the recession, based on data from the U.S. Census Bureau and the Bureau of Labor Statistics. Approximately, 1.3 million of these losses have occurred in the last four months. More than 320,000 Americans lost their employer-provided health insurance in March [2009] alone, which amounts to approximately 10,680 workers a day. . . .

All industries except four—natural resources and mining, utilities, education and health services, and government—saw declines in their payroll employment over the last 15 months.

Employees in the durable goods manufacturing sector bore the greatest burden of the losses in coverage with approximately 733,600 workers becoming uninsured since December 2007. Durable goods manufacturing is followed by professional and business services, where 553,200 workers lost employer-based coverage, and construction where another 385,800 workers have lost employer-based coverage since the recession began.

The worst losses have been in recent months. More than 1 million workers lost health care coverage in the first three months of 2009, which is 42 percent of the total losses since December 2007. Approximately, 268,400 more workers lost health care coverage in March 2009 than in March 2008. Month-by-month estimates of the rising number of uninsured demonstrate how the pace of contraction in the labor market has affected the number of people with health insurance.

The rapid loss of health coverage demonstrates the fundamental instability of health insurance protections in our current system and the need for comprehensive health reform.

More Men Have Lost Access to Health Care Coverage than Women

Men are more likely to have employer-provided health insurance than their female counterparts in industries where both men and women are employed. This, in conjunction with the fact that male-dominated industries such as construction and manufacturing have fared worse in this recession than female-dominated industries, has exacerbated the impact of job loss on health coverage. . . .

Approximately, 1.7 million men have lost employer-provided health insurance from their jobs as of February 2009, compared to approximately 396,800 women. . . .

The rapid loss of health coverage demonstrates the fundamental instability of health insurance protections in our current system and the need for comprehensive health reform. As President Barack Obama asserted in a White House forum in March, "Health care reform is no longer just a moral imperative, it is a fiscal imperative. . . . If we want to create jobs and rebuild our economy, then we must address the crushing cost of health care this year, in this administration." The time to deliver quality, affordable health care coverage to our nation's families is now. The American people cannot afford another missed opportunity.

People Without Health Insurance Are Not More Likely to Die

Megan McArdle

Megan McArdle is a libertarian blogger and the business and economics editor for the Atlantic.

Outside of the few states where it is illegal to deny coverage based on medical history, I am probably uninsurable. Though I'm in pretty good health, I have several latent conditions, including an autoimmune disease. If I lost the generous insurance that I have through the *Atlantic*, even the most charitable insurer might hesitate to take me on.

So I took a keen interest when, at the fervid climax of the health care debate in mid-December, a *Washington Post* blogger, Ezra Klein, declared that Senator Joseph Lieberman, by refusing to vote for a bill with a public option, was apparently "willing to cause the deaths of hundreds of thousands" of uninsured people in order to punish the progressives who had opposed his reelection in 2006. In the ensuing blog storm, conservatives condemned Klein's "venomous smear," while liberals solemnly debated the circumstances under which one may properly accuse one's opponents of mass murder.

But aside from an exchange between Matthew Yglesias of the [progressive] Center for American Progress and Michael Cannon of the [libertarian] Cato Institute, few people addressed the question that mattered most to those of us who cannot buy an individual insurance policy at any price—the question that was arguably the health care debate's most important: Was Klein *right*? If we lost our insurance, would this

Megan McArdle, "Myth Diagnosis: Everyone Knows That People Without Health Insurance Are More Likely to Die. But Are They?" *Atlantic*, March 2010. Reprinted by permission.

gargantuan new entitlement really be the only thing standing between us and an early grave?

Problems with Research on the Uninsured

Perhaps few people were asking, because the question sounds so stupid. Health insurance buys you health care. Health care is supposed to save your life. So if you don't have someone buying you health care, well, you can complete the syllogism.

Last year's national debate on health care legislation tended to dwell on either heart-wrenching anecdotes about costly, unattainable medical treatments, or arcane battles over how many people in the United States lacked insurance. Republicans rarely plumbed the connection between insurance and mortality, presumably because they would look foolish and heartless if they expressed any doubt about health insurance's benefits. It was politically safer to harp on the potential problems of government interventions—or, in extremis, to point out that more than half the uninsured were either affluent, lacking citizenship, or already eligible for government programs in which they hadn't bothered to enroll.

Quite possibly, lack of health insurance has no more impact on your health than lack of flood insurance.

Even Democratic politicians made curiously little of the plight of the uninsured. Instead, they focused on cost control, so much so that you might have thought that covering the uninsured was a happy side effect of really throttling back the rate of growth in Medicare spending. When progressive politicians or journalists did address the disadvantages of being uninsured, they often fell back on the same data Klein had used: a 2008 report from the Urban Institute that estimated that about 20,000 people were dying every year for lack of health insurance.

But when you probe that claim, its accuracy is open to question. Even a rough approximation of how many people die because of lack of health insurance is hard to reach. Quite possibly, lack of health insurance has no more impact on your health than lack of flood insurance.

Part of the trouble with reports like the one from the Urban Institute is that they cannot do the kind of thing we do to test drugs or medical procedures: divide people randomly into groups that do and don't have health insurance, and see which group fares better. Experimental studies like this would be tremendously expensive, and it's hard to imagine that they'd attract sufficient volunteers. Moreover, they might well violate the ethical standards of doctors who believed they were condemning the uninsured patients to a life nasty, brutish, and short.

So instead, researchers usually do what are called "observational studies": they take data sets that include both insured and uninsured people, and compare their health outcomes— usually mortality rates, because these are unequivocal and easy to measure. For a long time, two of the best studies were [PD] Sorlie et al. (1994), which used a large sample of census data from 1982 to 1985; and [P] Franks, [CM] Clancy, and [MR] Gold (1993), which examined a smaller but richer data set from the National Health and Nutrition Examination Survey, and its follow-up studies, between 1971 and 1987. The Institute of Medicine used the math behind these two studies to produce a 2002 report on an increase in illness and death from lack of insurance; the Urban Institute, in turn, updated those numbers to produce the figure that became the gold standard during the debate over health care reform.

The first thing one notices is that the original studies are a trifle elderly. Medicine has changed since 1987; presumably, so has the riskiness of going without health insurance. Moreover, the question of who had insurance is particularly dodgy: The studies counted as "uninsured" anyone who lacked insurance in the initial interview. But of course, not all of those people would have stayed uninsured—a separate study suggests that only about a third of those who reported being uninsured over a two-year time frame lacked coverage for the entire period. Most of the "uninsured" people probably got insurance relatively quickly, while some of the "insured" probably lost theirs. The effect of this churn could bias your results either way; the inability to control for it makes the statistics less accurate.

The uninsured generally have more health risks than the rest of the population. They are poorer, more likely to smoke, less educated, more likely to be unemployed, [and] more likely to be obese.

The bigger problem is that the uninsured generally have more health risks than the rest of the population. They are poorer, more likely to smoke, less educated, more likely to be unemployed, more likely to be obese, and so forth. All these things are known to increase your risk of dying, independent of your insurance status.

There are also factors we can't analyze. It's widely believed that health improves with social status, a quality that's hard to measure. Risk-seekers are probably more likely to end up uninsured, and also to end up dying in a car crash—but their predilection for thrills will not end up in our statistics. People who are suspicious of doctors probably don't pursue either generous health insurance or early treatment. Those who score low on measures of conscientiousness often have trouble keeping jobs with good health insurance—or following complicated treatment protocols. And so on.

The studies relied upon by the Institute of Medicine and the Urban Institute tried to control for some of these factors. But Sorlie et al.—the larger study—lacked data on things like smoking habits and could control for only a few factors, while

Franks, Clancy, and Gold, which had better controls but a smaller sample, could not, as an observational study, categorically exclude the possibility that lack of insurance has no effect on mortality at all.

Support for Another Conclusion

The possibility that no one risks death by going without health insurance may be startling, but some research supports it. Richard Kronick of the University of California at San Diego's Department of Family and Preventive Medicine, an adviser to the Clinton administration, recently published the results of what may be the largest and most comprehensive analysis yet done of the effect of insurance on mortality. He used a sample of more than 600,000, and controlled not only for the standard factors, but for how long the subjects went without insurance, whether their disease was particularly amenable to early intervention, and even whether they lived in a mobile home. In test after test, he found no significantly elevated risk of death among the uninsured.

This result is not, perhaps, as shocking as it seems. Health care heals, but it also kills. Someone who lacked insurance over the past few decades might have missed taking their Lipitor, but also their Vioxx or fen-phen. According to one estimate, 80,000 people a year are killed just by "nosocomial infections"—infections that arise as a result of medical treatment. The only truly experimental study on health insurance, a randomized study of almost 4,000 subjects done by RAND [Corporation] and concluded in 1982, found that increasing the generosity of people's health insurance caused them to use more health care, but made almost no difference in their health status.

If gaining insurance has a large effect on people's health, we should see outcomes improve dramatically between one's early and late 60s. Yet like the Kronick and RAND studies, analyses of the effect of Medicare, which becomes available to virtually everyone in America at the age of 65, show little benefit. In a recent review of the literature, Helen Levy of the University of Michigan and David Meltzer of the University of Chicago noted that the latest studies of this question "paint a surprisingly consistent picture: Medicare increases consumption of medical care and may modestly improve self-reported health but has no effect on mortality, at least in the short run."

The possibility that no one risks death by going without health insurance may be startling, but some research supports it.

Of course, that might be an indictment of programs like Medicare and Medicaid. Indeed, given the uncertainties about their impact on mortality rates—uncertainties that the results from Sorlie et al. don't resolve—it's possible that, by blocking the proposed expansion of health care through Medicare, Senator Lieberman, rather than committing the industrial-scale slaughter Klein fears, might not have harmed anyone at all. We cannot use one study to "prove" that having government insurance is riskier than having none. But we also cannot use a flawed and conflicting literature to "prove" that Lieberman was willing to risk the deaths of hundreds of thousands. Government insurance should have some effect, but if that effect is not large enough to be unequivocally evident in the data we have, it must be small.

Even if we did agree that insurance rarely confers significant health benefits, that would not necessarily undermine the case for a national health care program. The academics who question the mass benefits of expanding coverage still think that doing so improves outcomes among certain vulnerable subgroups, like infants and patients with HIV [human immunodeficiency virus]. Besides, a national health program has nonmedical benefits. Leaving tens of millions of Americans without health insurance violates our sense of equity—and leaves those millions exposed to the risk of mind-boggling medical bills.

But we should have had a better handle on the case for expanded coverage—and, more important, the evidence behind it—before we embarked on a year-long debate that divided our house against itself. Certainly, we should have had it before Congress voted on the largest entitlement expansion in 40 years. Unfortunately, most of us forgot to ask a fundamental question, because we were certain we already knew the answer. By the time we got around to challenging our assumptions, it was too late to do anything except scream at each other from the sidelines.

Most of the Uninsured Are Young, Healthy, and Financially Well-Off

Michael D. Tanner

Michael D. Tanner is a senior fellow at the Cato Institute, a libertarian think tank. He is coauthor of the book Healthy Competition: What's Holding Back Health Care and How to Free It.

No single topic drives the health care reform debate like the number of uninsured Americans, variously numbered in speeches and ads at 45 million, 46 million, 47 million, or even 50 million. Unfortunately, most of what we think we know about the uninsured is wrong.

For the record, according to the latest figures from the [US] Census Bureau, 45.6 million Americans currently lack health insurance. This is actually down slightly from the 47 million that were uninsured in 2006. However, those numbers don't tell the whole story.

Examining the Numbers

For example, roughly one-quarter of those counted as uninsured—12 million people—are eligible for Medicaid and the State Children's Health Insurance Program (SCHIP), but haven't enrolled. This includes 64 percent of all uninsured children, and 29 percent of parents with children. Since these people would be enrolled in those programs automatically if they went to the hospital for care, calling them uninsured is really a smoke screen.

Another 10 million uninsured "Americans" are, at least technically, not Americans. Approximately 5.6 million are illegal immigrants, and another 4.4 million are legal immigrants but not citizens.

Michael D. Tanner, "Who Are the Uninsured?" Originally appeared in Philadelphia Inquirer. Cato Institute, August 20, 2009. Reprinted by permission.

Nor are the uninsured necessarily poor. A new study by June O'Neill, former director of the Congressional Budget Office [CBO], found that 43 percent of the uninsured have incomes higher than 250 percent of the poverty level ($55,125 for a family of four). And slightly more than a third have incomes in excess of $66,000. A second study, by Mark Pauly of the University of Pennsylvania and [M.] Kate Bundorf of Stanford, concluded that nearly three-quarters of the uninsured could afford coverage but chose not to purchase it.

And most of the uninsured are young and in good health. According to the CBO, roughly 60 percent are under the age of 35, and fully 86 percent report that they are in good or excellent health.

Finally, when we hear about 45 million Americans without health insurance, it conjures up the notion that all of those are born without health insurance, die without health insurance, and are never insured in between. The reality is that most people without health insurance are uninsured for a relatively short period of time.

Most of what we think we know about the uninsured is wrong.

Only about 30 percent of the uninsured remain so for more than a year, approximately 16 percent for two years, and less than 2.5 percent for three years or longer. About half are uninsured for six months or less. Notably, because health insurance is too often tied to employment, the working poor who cycle in and out of the job market also cycle in and out of health insurance.

Other Solutions

None of this is to suggest that many of those without health insurance do not face severe hardship, or that we shouldn't try to expand health insurance coverage. But it does mean that we might be able to deal with this problem in a much more targeted way, rather than having a huge and expensive new government program.

For example, young, healthy, and well-off people might be more inclined to buy insurance if it cost less. That means ending regulations, like community rating, that increase the cost of insurance for younger and healthier workers; eliminating costly mandated benefits; and creating more competition by allowing people to purchase insurance across state lines.

Fully 86 percent [of the uninsured] report that they are in good or excellent health.

And if people are losing their insurance when they lose their jobs, we should move away from a health care system dominated by employer-provided health insurance. That means changing the tax treatment of health insurance.

The current system excludes the value of employer-provided insurance from a worker's taxable income. However, workers purchasing health insurance on their own must do so with after-tax dollars. This provides a significant tilt toward employer-provided insurance. Workers should receive a standard deduction, a tax credit, or, better still, large health savings accounts (HSAs) for the purchase of health insurance, regardless of whether they receive it through their job or purchase it on their own.

We can then look at those people who may need some kind of subsidy to better afford insurance.

Doctors know that if you don't get the diagnosis correct, you are not going to prescribe the right treatment. The same is true with health care reform. In trying to expand coverage to those who need it, let's make certain we understand the facts.

The Majority of Voters Say Cost, Not Lack of Coverage, Is the Biggest Health Care Problem

Rasmussen Reports

Rasmussen Reports is an electronic media company specializing in the collection, publication, and distribution of public opinion polling information.

Most voters still believe cost is the biggest problem with health care in America today, but most also think passage of the health care plan proposed by President [Barack] Obama and congressional Democrats will drive costs even higher.

Survey Findings

A new Rasmussen Reports national telephone survey finds that 54% rate cost as the biggest problem, a finding that has been consistent for months. In July of last year [2009], however, 61% felt that way.

Only 24% cite the lack of universal coverage as the biggest problem with health care. For 11%, the quality of care is their greatest concern, while two percent (2%) list inconvenience and scheduling problems. Ten percent (10%) are undecided. It's interesting to note that 56% of those who have health insurance view cost as the biggest problem. But among those who don't have health insurance, 40% list the lack of universal coverage as the biggest problem, while 41% view cost that way.

Rasmussen Reports, "54% Say Cost Is Biggest Problem with Health Care," March 21, 2010. Reprinted by permission.

Views About President Obama's Health Care Reforms

As the House prepares to vote today [March 21, 2010] on the president's health care plan, 41% of all voters nationally favor the plan, while 54% oppose it. These figures have changed very little for months.

Fifty-seven percent (57%) believe that if the plan passes, the cost of health care will go up. Only 17% believe the plan will achieve the stated goal of reducing the cost of care.

Only 24% [of Americans] cite the lack of universal coverage as the biggest problem with health care.

Fifty-five percent (55%) of voters think Congress should scrap the current health care plan and start all over again. Fifty percent (50%) say they are less likely to vote this November to reelect a member of Congress who votes for the health care plan. Voters ages 30 to 64 feel strongest that cost is the biggest problem with health care today. Sixty percent (60%) of married voters share that belief, compared to 41% of those who are not married.

Fifty-one percent (51%) of those who favor a single-payer health care system where the federal government provides coverage for everyone think lack of universal coverage is the biggest problem. Sixty-seven percent (67%) of those who oppose a single-payer system rate cost as the biggest problem.

Most Republicans and voters not affiliated with either major party have consistently opposed the health care plan, while most Democrats favor it. This is explained in part by the findings that 62% of GOP [Republican] voters and 57% of unaffiliateds think cost is the biggest problem with health care, while Democrats are narrowly divided over whether lack of universal coverage or cost is the greatest concern.

Forty-seven percent (47%) of all voters favor the portion of the plan that would spend "several hundred billion dollars over the coming decade to expand coverage of the uninsured." Fifty-one percent (51%) oppose it. This includes 28% who strongly favor and 38% who strongly oppose.

Forty-four percent (44%) now rate the U.S. health care system as good or excellent. That's up from 35% when the president first proposed his reform ideas last May and up from 29% two years ago.

Just 28% now say the U.S. health care system is poor. Additionally, 76% of those with health insurance rate their own coverage as good or excellent. The Congressional Budget Office says the proposed legislation will reduce the deficit over 10-years' time, but voters are skeptical of the official government projections. Eighty-one percent (81%) believe the health care plan will cost more than projected. That's one reason voters overwhelmingly believe passage of the plan will increase the deficit and is likely to mean higher middle-class taxes.

CHAPTER 2

Does Access to Health Insurance Improve People's Health?

Chapter Preface

The most common type of health insurance—for both people who have health insurance through their employers and those who are self-insured in the individual insurance market—is a managed care plan. A managed care plan is one in which insurance companies contract with doctors, hospitals, and other health care providers to provide care at a negotiated price. The goal of these plans is to control health care costs. The group of contracted medical providers is called the plan's network, and subscribers are either required or encouraged to use this network when they seek health care services. The two most popular managed care plans are health maintenance organizations (HMOs) and preferred provider organizations (PPOs).

HMOs are the most restrictive type of managed care. They require subscribers to choose doctors and other providers from within the plan's network and do not pay for services obtained from providers who have not agreed to be part of the HMO plan. Also, most HMOs require subscribers to select a primary care doctor who acts as a gatekeeper to coordinate each patient's health care. Subscribers, therefore, must get the primary care doctor's referral in order to have lab tests, X-rays, or other tests, or to see a specialist. Failure to secure a referral typically means that the subscriber must pay for the service out of pocket. HMOs were developed in the 1970s as a way to address rising health care costs, but they have become less popular than they once were, largely because of the many restrictions on patient choice of doctors and other services.

PPO insurance is a newer and faster-growing type of managed care plan, designed to give subscribers significantly more choices than HMO plans. PPOs work by creating a network of providers, similar to HMOs; but in a PPO, subscribers do not have to choose a primary care doctor and are not required to have referrals to have testing or other procedures or to see a specialist. PPO subscribers who see doctors and providers in the preferred network typically pay only a co-payment of $20 to $40 for each doctor's visit, but they are still responsible for fulfilling the annual deductible on their policies—that is, a set amount that must be paid out of pocket each year before insurance kicks in. PPO plans vary in terms of which medical services are subject to the deductible and which services are exempt from the deductible and available with only a co-pay. Usually, however, the amounts paid for medical services while fulfilling the deductible are negotiated prices that are lower than someone without insurance might be charged. If a PPO subscriber decides to obtain care from a doctor or provider not in the preferred network, the costs will be much higher and the subscriber must pay out of pocket and then file a claim with the PPO to be reimbursed for those services covered by the plan.

PPOs therefore provide much more flexibility, convenience, and patient choice than HMOs, but the downside is that they are usually more expensive, with higher premiums, co-payments, and deductibles. In fact, because health care costs have continued to explode in recent years, insurers and employers have encouraged subscribers to select PPO plans with higher and higher deductibles as a way of holding down premium costs (the monthly or bimonthly rate charged by the insurance company for the PPO plan). As a result, consumers, even those in managed care plans, are shouldering more and more of their health care costs.

Indeed, the average out-of-pocket health care costs for a typical family with a managed care plan can easily exceed $15,000 per year. According to the Kaiser Family Foundation, the average premium cost of a family health insurance policy offered by an employer was $13,375 in 2009, and policies for the self-insured ran even higher. If a self-insured family pays at least $13,375 in premiums, another $5,000 out of pocket for services subject to the deductible, and multiple co-pays for covered services adding up to around $1,000, that family would incur annual out-of-pocket costs of $19,375—almost the entire yearly earnings for families who meet the poverty guidelines of $22,050 for a family of four. Most health care experts, therefore, have concluded that managed care plans will not solve the problem of rising health care costs.

The rising cost of health insurance has caused some health experts to question the relationship between insurance and health. The viewpoints in this chapter address this issue of whether access to health insurance improves people's health.

Health Insurance Is Important to the Health and Well-Being of Both Children and Adults

Institute of Medicine

The Institute of Medicine is part of the US National Academy of Sciences, a group of more than six thousand of the nation's top scientists, engineers, and health professionals who provide independent advice to US policy makers.

When policy makers and researchers consider potential solutions to the crisis of uninsurance in the United States, the question of whether health insurance matters to health is often an issue. This question is far more than an academic concern. It is crucial that U.S. health care policy be informed with current and valid evidence on the consequences of uninsurance for health care and health outcomes, especially for the 45.7 million individuals without health insurance.

From 2001 to 2004, the Institute of Medicine (IOM) issued six reports, which concluded that being uninsured was hazardous to people's health and recommended that the nation move quickly to implement a strategy to achieve health insurance coverage for all.

The goal of this [viewpoint] is to inform the health reform policy debate—in 2009—with an up-to-date assessment of the research evidence. This [viewpoint] addresses three key questions: (1) What are the dynamics driving downward trends in health insurance coverage? (2) Is being uninsured harmful to the health of children and adults? (3) Are insured people affected by high rates of uninsurance in their communities?

The Institute of Medicine, "America's Uninsured Crisis: Consequences for Health and Health Care," February 2009, by the National Academy of Sciences, Courtesy of the National Academies Press, Washington, D.C. Reprinted with permission from Institute of Medicine.

A Downward Spiral for Health Insurance Coverage

A number of ominous signs point to a continuing decline in health insurance coverage in the United States. Health care costs and insurance premiums are growing substantially faster than the economy and family incomes. Rising health care costs and a severely weakened economy threaten not only employer-sponsored insurance, the cornerstone of private health coverage in the United States, but also threaten recent expansions in public coverage. There is no evidence to suggest that the trends driving loss of insurance coverage will reverse without concerted action.

Overall, fewer workers, particularly those with lower wages, are offered employer-sponsored insurance, and fewer among the workers that are offered such insurance can afford the premiums. Moreover, employment has shifted away from industries with traditionally high rates of coverage, such as manufacturing, to service jobs, such as wholesale and retail trades, with historically lower rates of coverage. In some industries, employers have relied more heavily on jobs without health benefits, including part-time and shorter-term employment, and contract and temporary jobs. In addition, early retirees are less likely to be offered retiree health insurance benefits than in the past.

The states and the federal government have increased substantially health insurance coverage among low-income children and, to a lesser degree, among adults in the last decade. While these coverage expansions have mitigated the overall numbers of uninsured, many states are now under extreme economic pressures to cut their recent expansions of public programs.

Americans without access to employer-sponsored health coverage, other sources of group health insurance, or public insurance must turn to the non-group health insurance market if they want to obtain coverage. For many people, non-

group coverage is prohibitively expensive or altogether un-
available. In most states, insurers may deny applicants for
non-group coverage completely; impose either a permanent or
temporary preexisting condition limitation on coverage; or
charge a higher premium based on health status, occupation,
and other personal characteristics.

There is a chasm between the health care needs of people
without *health insurance and access to effective health
care services.*

Coverage Matters

A robust body of well-designed, high-quality research provides compelling findings about the harms of being uninsured
and the benefits of gaining health insurance for both children
and adults. Despite the availability of some safety net services,
there is a chasm between the health care needs of people
without health insurance and access to effective health care
services. This gap results in needless illness, suffering, and
even death.

Research shows children benefit considerably from health
insurance. When children acquire health insurance:

- They are more likely to have access to a usual source of
  care; well-child care and immunizations to prevent future illness and monitor developmental milestones; prescription medications; appropriate care for asthma; and
  basic dental services.

- Serious childhood health problems are more likely to
  be identified early, and children with special health care
  needs are more likely to have access to specialists.

- They receive more timely diagnosis of serious health
  conditions, experience fewer avoidable hospitalizations,
  have improved asthma outcomes, and miss fewer days
  of school.

For adults *without* health insurance, the evidence shows:

- Men and women are much less likely to receive clinical preventive services that have the potential to reduce unnecessary morbidity and premature death.

- Chronically ill adults delay or forgo visits with physicians and clinically effective therapies, including prescription medications.

- Adults are more likely to be diagnosed with later-stage cancers that are detectable by screening or by contact with a clinician who can assess worrisome symptoms.

- Adults are more likely to die from trauma or other serious acute conditions, such as heart attacks or strokes.

- Adults with cancer, cardiovascular disease (including hypertension, coronary heart disease, and congestive heart failure), stroke, respiratory failure, chronic obstructive pulmonary disease (COPD), or asthma exacerbation, hip fracture, seizures, and serious injury are more likely to suffer poorer health outcomes, greater limitations in quality of life, and premature death.

The evidence also demonstrates that when adults acquire health insurance, many of the negative health effects of uninsurance are mitigated.

Research shows children benefit considerably from health insurance.

Communities at Risk

There are stark differences in community-level uninsurance rates across states, counties, and even areas within counties. In 2007, state-level uninsurance rates ranged from 6 percent in Massachusetts up to almost 28 percent in Texas. Across zip codes in Los Angeles County, uninsurance rates in the non-elderly population in 2005 ranged from 6 percent to 45 percent.

Evaluating the effects of community-level uninsurance rates on insured populations and health care delivery systems is challenging. Even when the rates of uninsurance are comparable, uninsurance may not affect all communities in the same way. The available research suggests that when community-level rates of uninsurance are relatively high, *insured* adults in those communities are more likely to have difficulties obtaining needed health care and to be less satisfied with the care they receive. For example, privately insured, working-age adults in areas of higher uninsurance are less likely to report having a place to go when sick, having had a doctor's visit or routine preventive care, and having seen a specialist when needed. They are also less likely to be satisfied with their choice of primary care and specialty physicians or to feel trust in their doctor's decisions.

Adults [without health insurance] are more likely to die from trauma or other serious acute conditions, such as heart attacks or strokes.

The specific contribution of uninsurance to these problems is not well established. Nevertheless, well-documented fault lines in local health care delivery are particularly vulnerable to the financial pressures that may be exacerbated by higher uninsurance. These pressures contribute to the tendency of providers and capital investments in health care facilities and technology to be concentrated in well-insured areas, the reluctance of specialists to assume on-call responsibilities for emergencies, and a cascade of interrelated hospital-based problems such as insufficient inpatient bed capacity, strained emergency services, and barriers to timely trauma care. These problems can only worsen existing disparities between communities in the supply of provider services and other health care resources and may have potentially serious implications for the quality and timeliness of care for insured people, as well as uninsured people, in these communities.

The current economic crisis and associated growth in unemployment will fuel further decline in the number of people with health insurance and likely intensify financial pressures on local health care delivery.

A Need for Action

In the 5 years since the IOM recommended action to achieve coverage for all Americans, there has been no comprehensive national effort to expand coverage to everyone. A severely weakened economy, rising health care and health insurance costs, growing unemployment, and declining employment-based health insurance coverage all provide evidence that the U.S. health insurance system is in a state of crisis.

There is a compelling case for action. Simply stated: Health insurance coverage matters. Expanding health coverage to all Americans is essential. Action to reduce health care expenditures and the rate of increase in per capita health care spending is also of paramount importance if health insurance coverage for all is to be achieved and sustained.

The committee does not believe that action should be delayed pending the development of a long-term approach to underlying health care costs. Given the demonstrated harms of not having health insurance for children and adults, the committee believes that action to achieve coverage improvements should proceed immediately.

Insurance Coverage Is Strongly Related to Better Health Outcomes

Jill Bernstein, Deborah Chollet, and Stephanie Peterson

Jill Bernstein is a senior health policy analyst at the Center for Studying Health System Change (HSC), a public policy research center. Deborah Chollet is a senior fellow, and Stephanie Peterson is a research analyst, at Mathematica Policy Research Inc., another policy research organization.

Insurance coverage is strongly related to better health outcomes for both children and adults when it makes health care affordable and helps consumers use care appropriately. This [viewpoint] looks at how insurance improves health outcomes by helping people obtain preventive and screening services, prescription drug benefits, mental health and other services, and by improving continuity of care. Vulnerable populations are especially at risk of poor health outcomes when they are uninsured. Insurance coverage can also improve social and economic well-being, by averting developmental problems in children, increasing workforce productivity, decreasing use of hospital services, and reducing costs of public programs.

Uninsured Have Worse Health Outcomes

Uninsured people generally receive much less care, either preventive or for acute and chronic conditions, than insured people. In particular, uninsured adults report lower levels of self-perceived wellness and functioning. Estimating the number of premature deaths attributable to lack of insurance pre-

Jill Bernstein, Deborah Chollet, and Stephanie Peterson, "How Does Insurance Coverage Improve Health Outcomes?" Mathematica Policy Research Inc., April 2010. Reprinted by permission.

sents methodological challenges, but some research indicates that as many as 44,500 deaths per year in the United States are linked to lack of insurance.

Research on the use of preventive services, which has focused separately on children and adults, suggests that:

- Uninsured young children have lower immunization rates than insured children.

- Uninsured adults are less likely than insured adults to receive preventive services or screenings, such as mammograms, Pap smears, or prostate screening. In turn, inadequate prevention and screening increase the likelihood of preventable illness, missed diagnoses, and delays in treatment.

When uninsured people seek emergency care for severe illness or injury, their health outcomes generally are poorer—whether they are children or adults. For example:

- Uninsured children are 70 percent less likely than insured children to receive medical care for common childhood conditions, such as sore throat, or for emergencies, such as a ruptured appendix.

- When hospitalized, uninsured children are at greater risk of dying than children with insurance.

- Uninsured adults are 20 percent less likely than insured adults to receive care following an automobile accident and are at greater risk of death.

- At-risk adults without insurance have higher rates of stroke and greater risk of death than at-risk adults with insurance.

- Adult stroke victims without insurance are more likely to have neurological impairment and longer hospital stays, and are at greater risk of dying, than adult stroke victims with insurance.

People with chronic illnesses who lack insurance have limited access to both health care services and effective care management. In addition, children with special health care needs who do not have adequate insurance coverage are more likely to go without needed care. For example:

- Parents of uninsured children are more likely to report unmet needs for mental health services for their children. Uninsured children are also less likely to receive treatment for chronic conditions such as diabetes and asthma.

- Uninsured children have less access to a usual source of care, community-based services, and services to make transitions to adulthood.

Undiagnosed and untreated illnesses and conditions can result in costs to both individuals and society.

Because uninsured people are less likely to have a usual source of care, they generally have poorer control of chronic conditions, such as hypertension [high blood pressure]. Even when they are aware that they have a chronic condition, uninsured adults are less likely than adults who are insured to have a usual source of care or regular checkups. As a result, they have more emergency department visits and report greater short-term reductions in health; if they return to full health, they take longer to do so.

The prognosis for uninsured cancer patients also is worse than that for insured patients. In general, uninsured cancer patients die sooner after diagnosis, largely because they are less likely to be diagnosed in early stages of the disease. However, even when diagnosed at similar stages, uninsured patients with certain types of cancer die sooner than insured patients.

Lack of Insurance Affects Everyone

Undiagnosed and untreated illnesses and conditions can result in costs to both individuals and society. For example:

- Untreated health conditions cause uninsured children to lose opportunities for normal development. Their educational achievement suffers because they miss more days of school.

- Workers who are uninsured throughout the course of a year have a greater likelihood of missing work.

- Poorer health, greater disability, and premature death among uninsured workers have economic consequences for their families, employers, and the overall economy. The economic cost of lost productivity is substantial, especially when added to the costs of avoidable health care.

At a broader level, health providers and investors may find communities with a high proportion of uninsured residents less attractive locations than more affluent and better-insured communities. As a result, even people with insurance may have difficulty obtaining needed care in communities with relatively high rates of uninsured residents, and they may be less satisfied with the care they receive.

Coverage Features Matter

Many Americans are insured intermittently and, when insured, not all have coverage that is equally comprehensive. The research literature has associated continuous and comprehensive coverage with better health outcomes.

Continuous coverage. Disruptions in insurance coverage have been associated with less access to care, lower service use, and increases in unmet medical needs. Lapses and gaps in coverage also contribute to health disparities for people with low educational attainment and for the poor. Conversely, adults with continuous insurance coverage are healthier and at lower risk for premature death than those who are uninsured or whose coverage is intermittent, while children with continuous coverage are more likely to visit a doctor, receive preventive care, and have prescriptions filled.

Uninsured people generally receive much less care, either preventive or for acute and chronic conditions, than insured people.

Continuous coverage also can reduce administrative costs. For example, guaranteed eligibility for Medicaid and the Children's Health Insurance Program (CHIP) for 6 or 12 months can lower states' administrative costs by reducing the frequent movement (called "churning") of eligible individuals in and out of Medicaid and CHIP programs. Greater stability in plan membership also makes it easier to attract managed care plans to participate, which in turn can improve enrollees' access to care.

Coverage of preventive services. Ensuring access to the full range of appropriate and effective preventive services is essential for conferring the full health benefits of insurance coverage. Coverage for preventive services can reduce racial and ethnic disparities in health outcomes.

Coverage of prescription drugs. Limited coverage and high out-of-pocket costs for medication are associated with a decline in older adults' self-reported health status. Adults with certain chronic conditions who restrict their medications because of cost increase their risk of heart attacks and strokes. Low-income adults are especially likely to fail to comply with drug regimens because of cost. Conversely, adults with chronic conditions are more likely to follow drug regimens when they have insurance that covers prescription drugs.

Coverage of mental health services. Adults with health insurance that covers mental health services are more likely to receive mental health treatment that is consistent with medical guidelines. In particular, receiving care for depression improves outcomes. When uninsured, people with mental illness rely heavily on emergency room services, with significant costs to the community.

Affordable cost sharing. Health insurance helps people establish and maintain access to appropriate care, which can lead to better outcomes. High cost sharing (including deductibles, coinsurance, and co-payments) can create barriers to obtaining care, reducing necessary service use among those who are insured.

Considerations for Policy Makers

The Patient Protection and Affordable Care Act enacted in March 2010 seeks to expand coverage immediately and over the long term. It establishes a temporary, national high-risk pool to provide coverage for individuals denied insurance in the individual market. It creates incentives for the formation of nonprofit Consumer Operated and Oriented Plans (CO-OPs) to compete with existing insurers as early as 2012. By 2014, the states will create health insurance exchanges that guarantee coverage for all individuals and small businesses, and Medicaid eligibility will be extended to all residents with income below 133 percent of the federal poverty level (FPL). With few exceptions, all individuals will be required to have coverage that qualifies as "an essential health benefits package."

The new law acknowledges that health insurance leads to better outcomes when it makes health care affordable and helps consumers use care appropriately. By 2011, all health plans must cover at least the preventive services rated A or B by the U.S. Preventive Services Task Force as well as recommended immunizations; preventive care for infants, children, and adolescents; and additional preventive care and screenings for women. Plans may not impose cost sharing for these services. In addition, preventive and wellness services, chronic disease management, and mental health and drug benefits are included in the essential benefit package that will constitute minimum required coverage in 2014.

In implementing the new law, federal and state policy makers should consider lessons learned about continuous coverage and affordable care. For example, cost sharing, especially for mental health and drug benefits, can create financial barriers that jeopardize the appropriate and efficient use of care. Policy makers might also consider ways to make it easier for populations enrolled in public programs and coverage through the exchanges, particularly populations with serious conditions or special needs, to maintain relationships with their primary care providers over time.

Not Having Health Insurance Increases the Risk of Cancer Death

Walter Jessen

Walter Jessen is a cancer neurobiologist and bioinformatician, as well as the founder, editor, and head writer of Highlight HEALTH, a health-related website.

With all the recent discussion and debate by the presidential candidates regarding health care issues, I thought a study published last month [December 2007] in *CA: A Cancer Journal for Clinicians* was quite timely. The study, titled "Association of Insurance with Cancer Care Utilization and Outcomes," presents evidence that lack of adequate health insurance coverage is associated with reduced access to care and poorer outcomes for cancer patients. The article further presents data on the association between health insurance status and screening, stage at diagnosis and survival for breast and colorectal cancer.

American Cancer Society (ACS) researchers analyzed over half a million patient cases using data from the National Cancer Data Base as well as data from the 2005 and 2006 National Health Interview Survey conducted by the National Center for Health Statistics and the Centers for Disease Control and Prevention (CDC). Perhaps not surprisingly, the results show that uninsured individuals are (1) less likely to receive cancer screening, (2) more likely to be diagnosed at an advanced disease stage and (3) less likely to survive than privately insured individuals.

Walter Jessen, "Lack of Health Insurance Increases Risk of Cancer Death," Highlight HEALTH, January 7, 2008. Reprinted by permission.

National Health Survey and Health Care

People who are uninsured or insured by government programs may face significant obstacles obtaining health care. Indeed, some physicians do not accept new patients without private insurance or uninsured individuals who are not able to pay the full cost at the time of visit. A recent national survey found that while 96% of office-based physicians were currently accepting new patients, 40.3% indicated they would not accept new charity cases, 25.5% did not accept new Medicaid cases and 13.9% did not accept new Medicare cases. This lack of access to health care can have adverse effects on preventive care and management for chronic conditions.

In the present ACS study, analyses of the 2006 National Health Interview Survey showed that 53.6% of uninsured people aged 18 to 64 years had no usual source of health care compared to just 9.9% of privately insured and 10.8% of individuals with Medicaid insurance. People who are uninsured were much more likely to report no health care visits in the past year than people who are privately or Medicaid insured. Compared to insured individuals, people who were uninsured were more likely to report that they did not get care due to cost, delayed care due to cost, did not get prescription drugs due to cost and had no health care visits in the past 12 months due to cost.

Some physicians do not accept new patients without private insurance or uninsured individuals who are not able to pay the full cost at the time of visit.

National Health Survey and Cancer Prevention

Up to two-thirds of cancers may be prevented through healthy lifestyle changes. Health care visits provide an opportunity for health providers to counsel people on smoking cessation and weight loss. However, uninsured individuals are much more likely to report no health care visits in the past 12 months than people who are Medicaid or privately insured and are thus much less likely to be advised to quit smoking or to lose weight. Further, analyses of the 2006 National Health Interview Survey showed that the likelihood of receiving recommended cancer screening tests varied by insurance status. Privately insured women were most likely to have had a mammogram or Pap test, followed by Medicaid-insured women. Similarly, privately insured men were most likely to have had a test for prostate cancer, followed by Medicaid-insured men. Further, both men and women who were privately insured were most likely to have had a colorectal cancer screening test. In all cases, uninsured individuals were least likely to have had any type of cancer screening.

Health insurance status is associated with other sociodemographic characteristics (e.g., race, level of education). However, when the data was analyzed by race, at every level of education, individuals with health insurance were about twice as likely as those without to have had mammography or colorectal cancer screening. Thus, having health insurance is an important predictor of cancer screening.

Insurance Status, Cancer Stage at Diagnosis and Survival

ACS researchers also analyzed data from the National Cancer Data Base to investigate the relationship between insurance status, cancer stage at diagnosis and survival. In analyses of cancer survival for all cancers, uninsured individuals and Medicaid-insured individuals were 1.6 times more likely to die in five years than those with private insurance. Specifically, 35% of uninsured patients died in five years compared with 23% of privately insured patients. Since cancer screening tests are key to diagnosing and treating cancer in its early stages, not surprisingly people with health insurance were more likely to be diagnosed with early stage disease than individuals without insurance.

These results are consistent with previous studies showing that people who are uninsured or have Medicaid insurance are more likely to be diagnosed with late-stage cancer (breast and cancer of the mouth or throat, respectively) than people who are privately insured.

According to Dr. Otis Brawley, chief medical officer of the American Cancer Society:

> This report clearly suggests that insurance and cost-related barriers to care are critical to address if we want to ensure that all Americans are able to share in the progress we have achieved by having access to high-quality cancer prevention, early detection, and treatment services.

Research has shown that healthy lifestyle changes can prevent cancer. Additionally, advances in cancer detection and treatment have resulted in a decline in US cancer deaths in 2003 and 2004, the first decrease seen since 1930.

In analyses of cancer survival for all cancers, uninsured individuals and Medicaid-insured individuals were 1.6 times more likely to die in five years than those with private insurance.

The American Cancer Society launched the Access to Care campaign in 2007. Access to Care is a national initiative dedicated to raising awareness about the predicament of uninsured and underinsured people in the United States. The campaign encourages Americans to find ways to fix the problem and make access to health care a national priority.

Health Insurance and More Medical Care Do Not Necessarily Produce Health Benefits

Maggie Mahar

Maggie Mahar is the health care fellow at the Century Foundation, a policy research institution. She is the author of the book Money-Driven Medicine: The Real Reason Health Care Costs So Much.

Do the uninsured die because they don't have access to medical care—or because more than three-quarters of the uninsured are poor? . . . We know that poverty is a killer. It destroys mind and body, slowly but surely. In the U.S. the poor die seven years earlier than the rich. And most of the uninsured are poor.

I also [have] explained that lack of access to medical care is not a major factor in determining who dies prematurely. Social circumstances, personal behaviors, and environment account for 60% of early deaths, and each is closely tied to socioeconomic status.

Health Insurance and Health

Most Americans assume that good health care is the key to longevity. But in 2002 the Kaiser Family Foundation published a study that poses a radical question, "Does having health insurance improve your health?" It might sound like a foolish query. One wants to say "Of course!"

But early in the report, the authors acknowledge that "there is no definitive research that unambiguously answers this question, one way or the other."

Maggie Mahar, "Does Health Insurance Save Lives? Maybe That's the Wrong Question," *Taking Note* (blog), February 19, 2010. Reprinted by permission of Maggie Mahar, the Century Foundation.

Are We Overestimating the Importance of Medical Care?

They explain why: "An ideal study designed to answer it would randomly assign a representative sample of people to insured (treatment) and uninsured (control) groups. People in the treatment group would presumably use more medical care than people in the control group because having insurance lowers the cost of care.

"The extra services used by the insured might be a mix of more preventive care; more screening and diagnostic care designed to detect disease at an early, more treatable phase; and more aggressive treatment of illness when it occurs. Some people without insurance would find such treatments unaffordable and choose to forego care. If these are the effects of having insurance, then we might very well expect the insured group to have better health after some period of time.

"But," the report continues, "Suppose instead that the extra care received by the insured group was primarily medical services that were unneeded and provided little clinical benefit. . . . Suppose also that people without insurance are generally able to get care when they really need it. . . ."

In other words, while the uninsured do not receive the chronic disease management that they need, when they become seriously ill, they wind up in an emergency room where, most of the time, they are rescued.

In the U.S. the poor die seven years earlier than the rich.

When researchers try to investigate the benefit of having insurance and easy access to medical care, they run into another complication: If you look at the effect of additional medical care on healthy, well-insured peopled you find little or no benefit. For example, while the well-known RAND Health Insurance Experiment showed that low or no co-pays increases the amount of medical care people consume, "for the average person there were no substantial benefits from free care."

However, as the authors of the Kaiser study point out, the problem of being uninsured is not, by and large, a problem for "the average American—it is primarily a problem for low-income people." *And precisely because low-income people are sicker than average, they need more medical care.*

The authors of the Kaiser report conclude: "Even if one accepts as valid the findings of the more methodologically sound studies that suggest little or no health benefit from additional medical care use by well-insured populations, it does not necessarily follow that the uninsured would not benefit both from health insurance coverage and from greater medical care use. Holding both points of view would not be inconsistent. In fact, it would seem to be both inappropriate and unfair to argue on the basis of these studies that the uninsured should be penalized, i.e., denied help in obtaining insurance coverage, because of the inefficient or excessive use of medical care by the well insured.

When [the uninsured] become seriously ill, they wind up in an emergency room where, most of the time, they are rescued.

"Even if the marginal benefit [of more care] to the average, relatively healthy, privately insured person is close to zero, it does not follow that the benefit is also zero for a poor patient."

The Uninsured Are More Likely to Die of Specific Diseases—but Why?

Studies of outcomes from specific diseases (breast cancer, colorectal cancer, cardiovascular disease, and trauma) reveal that the odds of dying within a particular time period were from about 1.2 to 2.1 times greater for an uninsured person with the particular condition compared to a privately insured person. We also know that the uninsured tend to be diagnosed later.

But they still can't answer the question of causality: Do tens of thousands of uninsured people die because they weren't diagnosed in time? Or did they die because they were poor as well as uninsured—and thus not as strong as more affluent patients who managed to survive a heart attack or cancer?

In the end, studies linking the lack of insurance to mortality are inconclusive. "These studies vary in how they report their results, some as relative odds, some as relative risk ratios, and others as elasticities," the authors of the Kaiser study acknowledge. Taking these differences into account, their estimates of the quantitative effect of extending health insurance coverage to all suggest that "the mortality rates of the uninsured would declined by at least 5% and, depending on age and medical condition, by as much as 20–25%, with some studies suggesting that the reduction could be as high as 50%."

In essence, they are saying that "while we are quite certain that access to care must benefit patients, we have absolutely no idea how large that benefit is."

The Wrong Question

Ultimately, when people ask, "How many lives would be saved if we all had insurance?" I think they are posing the wrong question.

A better question would be: "How many people suffer needlessly because they don't have access to care?"

Why should "mortalities" be the measure of how much good health insurance—or medicine itself—can do? Health care will not rescue us from the human condition. And as I explained ..., evidence shows that access to medical care is not the major factor that guards against premature death. Genes, social circumstances and personal behavior all are far more important.

Despite our national obsession with longevity, and our belief that hi-tech medicine will rescue us, the truth is that very often, modern medicine cannot cure us—but it can provide comfort and care. This is why health insurance is important.

Whether the patient is a child with an earache, a 60-year-old who should have a knee replacement, or a chronically depressed 40-year-old, good insurance can provide access to the help they need. In a life-threatening situation, the uninsured may well get the emergency care that they need. But 21st-century medicine can greatly enhance the quality of life; this is why everyone deserves access.

Access to medical care is not the major factor that guards against premature death.

Richard Kronick agrees. . . . I explained [in an earlier post] that when he adjusts for demographic differences Kronick finds no evidence that an uninsured smoker dies sooner than a smoker who is insured. But he explained to PolitiFact.com, "he doesn't doubt that individuals' health suffers when they're uninsured." "No one would choose not to have insurance if they could afford it," Kronick added, "There's no benefit to having 47 million Americans uninsured."

Yet there is a limit to what insurance can do. It cannot create jobs. Or safe playgrounds. Or urban farms on inner-city roofs. It cannot reduce class sizes in our public schools. It cannot build preschools. If we are interested in reducing the level of premature deaths in this country, we must invest in public health. This means focusing on the poor.

As [SA] Schroeder pointed out in the 2007 Shattuck Lecture: "To the extent that the United States has a health strategy, its focus is on the development of new medical technologies and support for basic biomedical research. We already lead the world in the per capita use of most diagnostic and therapeutic medical technologies, and we have recently doubled the budget for the National Institutes of Health. . . . It is arguable that the status quo is an accurate expression of the national political will—a relentless search for better health among the middle and upper classes."

Schroeder notes that few lobbyists represent the poor: "The disadvantaged are less well represented in the political sphere here than in most other developed countries, which often have an active labor movement and robust labor parties. Without a strong voice from Americans of low socioeconomic status, citizen health advocacy in the United States coalesces around particular illnesses, such as breast cancer, human immunodeficiency virus [HIV] infection and acquired immunodeficiency syndrome (AIDS), and autism. These efforts are led by middle-class advocates whose lives have been touched by the disease. There have been a few successful public advocacy campaigns on issues of population health—efforts to ban exposure to secondhand smoke or to curtail drunk driving—but such efforts are relatively uncommon. Because the biggest gains in population health will come from attention to the less well-off, little is likely to change unless they have a political voice and use it to argue for more resources to improve health-related behaviors, reduce social disparities, increase access to health care, and reduce environmental threats. . . . In addition, the American emphasis on the value of individual responsibility creates a reluctance to intervene in what are seen as personal behavioral choices."

Yes, without question, we need health care reform. But neither Aetna [an insurance company] nor a single-payer system will save tens of thousands of lives. To do that, we need a war on poverty. Schroeder suggests that in "the absence of a strong political voice from the less fortunate themselves, it is incumbent on health care professionals, especially physicians, to become champions for population health. . . . Americans take great pride in asserting that we are number one in terms of wealth, number of Nobel Prizes, and military strength. Why don't we try to become number one in health?"

The Lack of Health Care Is Not Responsible for Low US Life Expectancy

Ronald Bailey

Ronald Bailey is a science correspondent for Reason *magazine and Reason.com, where he writes a weekly science and technology column.*

The mantra of would-be health care reformers is that the U.S. spends much more on health care than other industrialized countries, yet America ranks below average on major health indicators, including infant mortality and life expectancy.

Well, yes. Reformers generally imply that our dysfunctional and expensive health care system is to blame. Not so fast, say University of Pennsylvania demographers Samuel Preston and Jessica Ho. In a recent study they conclude:

> Life expectancy in the United States fares poorly in international comparisons, primarily because of high mortality rates above age 50. Its low ranking is often blamed on a poor performance by the health care system rather than on behavioral or social factors. This paper presents evidence on the relative performance of the US health care system using death avoidance as the sole criterion. We find that, by standards of OECD [Organisation for Economic Co-operation and Development] countries, the US does well in terms of screening for cancer, survival rates from cancer, survival rates after heart attacks and strokes, and medication of individuals with high levels of blood pressure or cholesterol. We consider in greater depth mortality from prostate cancer and breast cancer, diseases for which effective methods of

Ronald Bailey, "Is Lack of Government Health Care Responsible for Low U.S. Life Expectancy?," *Reason*, September 22, 2009. Reprinted by permission of Reason magazine and Reason.com.

identification and treatment have been developed and where behavioral factors do not play a dominant role. We show that the US has had significantly faster declines in mortality from these two diseases than comparison countries. We conclude that the low longevity ranking of the United States is not likely to be a result of a poorly functioning health care system.

Citing the Preston and Ho study, *New York Times* science journalist John Tierney notes:

> But there are many more differences between Europe and the United States than just the health care system. Americans are more ethnically diverse. They eat different food. They are fatter. Perhaps most important, they used to be exceptionally heavy smokers. For four decades, until the mid-1980s, per capita cigarette consumption was higher in the United States (particularly among women) than anywhere else in the developed world. Dr. Preston and other researchers have calculated that if deaths due to smoking were excluded, the United States would rise to the top half of the longevity rankings for developed countries.

The low longevity ranking of the United States is not likely to be a result of a poorly functioning health care system.

Back in 2008, I cited some of the same evidence and arguments in my column, "Accidents, Murders, Preemies, Fat, and U.S. Life Expectancy." After listing our many unhealthy proclivities, I optimistically concluded:

> Taking all these unhealthy proclivities into consideration, the American health care system is most likely not to blame for our lower life expectancies. Instead, American health care is rescuing enough of us from the consequences of our bad health habits to keep our ranking from being even lower.

To repeat, Preston and Ho conclude:

The question that we have posed is much simpler: Does a poor performance by the US health care system account for the low international ranking of longevity in the US? Our answer is, "no".

High Deductibles and Benefit Limits Can Diminish Health Care Coverage, Even for the Insured

Drew Altman

Drew Altman is president and chief executive officer of the Kaiser Family Foundation, a nonprofit, private foundation that focuses on major health care issues facing the United States and the US role in global health policy.

Our group that works on health care cost issues just updated an analysis that sheds light on what's really happening to people in the individual health insurance market, the issue Secretary [Kathleen] Sebelius, a former Kansas insurance commissioner, and others have put in the spotlight by calling on Anthem and other insurance companies to account for their proposed high premium increases. The analysis shows that people buying health insurance on their own in the individual market from 2004–2007 still paid 52% of their health expenses, on average, out of their own pockets. In other words, people bought insurance and paid premiums and still on average paid for about half of their health costs themselves. This compares with a much lower out-of-pocket share for employer-sponsored coverage of 30%.

High Premiums and Higher Deductibles

This points to what has really been going on in the individual insurance market. There has recently been a great deal of focus on increases in individual insurance premiums such as the

Drew Altman, "When Premiums Go Up 39%," Kaiser Family Foundation, March 10, 2010. This information was reprinted with permission from the Henry J. Kaiser Family Foundation. The Kaiser Family Foundation is a non-profit private operating foundation, based in Menlo Park, California, dedicated to producing and communicating the best possible analysis and information on health issues.

proposed Anthem increase in our home state [California]. Such premium increases are eye-popping and greater scrutiny by regulators is appropriate. But there is another phenomenon in the non-group market even more pervasive than large premium hikes; it's what is known in the industry as "buy-downs." When insurers inform members of large premium hikes, they commonly suggest that the increase can be mitigated (or sometimes even eliminated) by switching to a lower cost policy (which means a policy with higher deductibles and/or greater limits on benefits). Data from eHealthInsurance.com bear this out: The average deductible for family plans in the individual market increased from $2,760 in 2008 to $3,128 in 2009—just one year later. After years of these buy-downs, you end up with what we found in our recent analysis; insurance that, on average, pays for only about half of people's health care bills.

People buying health insurance on their own in the individual market from 2004–2007 still paid 52% of their health expenses, on average, out of their own pockets.

The trend is not unique to the individual market. We've experienced this choice ourselves on several occasions as a modestly sized employer. Our annual employer survey has been documenting steady increases in high deductible plans for several years, especially in smaller firms where the percentage of workers in plans with very high deductibles increased from 16% in 2006 to 40% in 2009. All this underscores a basic point: Rising health care costs and insurance company practices are leading not just to more expensive premiums, but to skimpier, less comprehensive coverage as well; slowly redefining what we have known as health insurance. To be sure, some economists argue that this is precisely what should happen, that people should have more "skin in the game." But this is not likely how regular people see it. Appropriate cost sharing is one thing, but we may be reaching the point in the individual market where the policies many people have simply cannot be considered meaningful coverage.

Health Care Reform

These data also provide some context for the discussion at the recent health care summit about what would happen to insurance premiums under reform. The Congressional Budget Office (CBO) has estimated that individual insurance premiums would, on average, go up under reform because people will be buying better coverage. That's not too surprising when you look at the kind of skimpy insurance people buying on their own often have today. In fact, for equivalent coverage, the CBO estimates that premiums under reform would be somewhat lower than under the status quo. And some would qualify for tax credits that would provide substantial premium relief as well.

The average deductible for family plans in the individual market increased from $2,760 in 2008 to $3,128 in 2009—just one year later.

But, affordability goes beyond what people pay in premiums. Ultimately, people may end up focusing as much, if not more, on their deductibles (the share of their health expenses they have to pay before their insurance kicks in). Deductibles are not only understandable to most people, but they are important for health access and economic security as well. If they are too high, they can be a disincentive to get care, especially for the chronically ill, and a burden on family budgets. To date, the discussion of affordability in health reform has focused mainly on premiums and not as much on the bigger picture of total out-of-pocket costs, including deductibles and cost sharing. In President [Barack] Obama's recent health care proposal, he notably improves on the affordability of the Senate health care bill; both in terms of premiums and out-of-pocket costs.

The recent premium increases in the individual market probably have done more to illustrate the cost of doing nothing in health reform in simple, graphic terms people can understand than anything so far in the health reform debate. However, as we follow the debate about proposed Anthem-like increases in the individual market, it is important to remember that the burden of those increases is felt not only in higher premiums, but often in less comprehensive health insurance coverage.

Expanded Access to Health Insurance Is Not the Only Tool to Improve Population Health

Harold Pollack

Harold Pollack is the Helen Ross Professor at the School of Social Service Administration at the University of Chicago and a special correspondent for the New Republic.

[Commentators] Megan McArdle and Ezra Klein (and friends) are duking it out over the potential impact of universal health insurance coverage on mortality. [Journalist] Jonathan Cohn has already weighed in, but I wanted to add my two cents.

It's useful to divide this controversy into two separate questions. First, does health insurance improve health, and if so, how, and by how much? Second, what else do we need to do?

Health Insurance and Improving Health

The first question occasions a very old argument. It's easy to swing widely between cynicism and naïveté. Although every one of us will eventually die, mortality is a rare and complicated event within almost every medical or social science study. Death occurs from multiple causes that unfold over a long period of time. It is difficult to tease out these interrelated causes.

Two excellent recent studies reached quite different results in exploring this question. The Institute of Medicine planted its flag roughly at the midpoint, implying that roughly 22,000

Harold Pollack, "Will Lack of Insurance Kill You?" *New Republic*, February 18, 2010. Reprinted by permission of THE NEW REPUBLIC, © 2010.

Americans die every year because they are uncovered. The large accompanying uncertainties in this literature don't indicate that health insurance isn't valuable. They indicate that it is hard to know when and why such coverage really matters.

The cynical case is surprisingly easy to make. Uninsured people are not randomly selected from the general population. Their heightened risks for various bad outcomes, including mortality, may reflect aspects of their own behavior and circumstances that are not caused by the lack of insurance coverage. Catapulting insurance cards to every American cannot address many social, economic, and even medical determinants of health. Robert Schoeni, James House, George Kaplan, and I co-edited a rather large tome which explores this theme.

There is also the awkward fact that much medical care is of no proven value. With dismaying frequency, such proof is lacking because the care is of no genuine value at all. Many of us are overinsured, which is one valid reason to tax Cadillac insurance plans.

Even when health care really matters, there are backdoor ways to finance health care for the uninsured. Consider what happens to uninsured breast cancer patients. Many present at later disease stages and require urgent and costly care. Faced with such an emergency, providers scramble, and often find some way to provide this care, often at a county hospital or another safety-net provider. (These same providers may then send a whopping bill, or they may foist the cost of her care onto the hospital or onto others, but that's another matter.)

Popular impressions of the thirty-year-old RAND Health Insurance Experiment [HIE]—possibly the most important true policy experiment ever done—reinforces the cynical view. The RAND HIE was far from perfect. Nobody was actually uninsured. Indeed the high-deductible plan was surprisingly comprehensive by year-2010 standards. The experiment was short, three years for most participants, and five years for the others. Still the results were striking and appear supported by many later studies. People assigned to free care received 40 percent more services than those assigned to a high-deductible plan. Yet the typical person enrolled in the free-care group was not tangibly healthier. You can see where McArdle and others might be skeptical given such results.

Much medical care is of no proven value.

A close reading of the RAND study and of many others, should dispel the skepticism. The RAND study predicted that low-income patients enrolled in a high-deductible plan would experience a 38 percent higher mortality rate than their otherwise comparable peers enrolled in a free-care plan. Almost all of this difference reflected differences in hypertension [high blood pressure]—a special killer within minority communities throughout the United States.

Health studies based on Medicare tell a similar story. I've written in this space before about the impressive body of work produced by [J. Michael] McWilliams and colleagues. These authors document marked improvement in many health measures at age 65 when individuals become Medicare eligible. They also document important reductions in race/ethnic and educational disparities in hypertension and blood glucose control. At age 65, racial disparities in systolic blood pressure decreased by 60 percent. Educational and race/ethnic disparities in blood glucose control decreased by more than 75 percent. Educational disparities in total cholesterol levels became negligible.

For these and other outcomes, important health disparities markedly decline once people join the essentially universal Medicare system. Medicare could do a much better job in addressing hypertension, diabetes, and other chronic diseases. Indeed the House and Senate health reform bills both include important measures to promote preventive care and improve disease management. Yet this is a substantial achievement. It's too bad that Americans must reach age 65 to receive this benefit. It's doubly too bad that our over-65 population shows such tenuous commitment to providing other Americans with the same financial and health security.

But these are political rather than epidemiological questions. Does health insurance save lives? Almost certainly it does, though the size and the causal pathways of the protective effect remain uncertain. Should we continue epidemiological research to pin down these relationships and improve other, noninsurance strategies to save lives? Absolutely.

On this first money question, then, would universal coverage make people tangibly healthier? You betcha.

Other Options for Improving Health

In addressing the second question, McArdle's skepticism deserves a more sympathetic hearing. Suppose we accept that universal coverage could save 22,000 lives every year. That's a large number, but there are other ways to save thousands of lives that are much more cost effective than expanding health insurance coverage. We systematically neglect these other opportunities.

Americans often conflate the challenge of improving population health with the challenge of assuring universal access to health care, which we further conflate with universal access to personal medical services through public or private insurance coverage. Each link of this causal chain is open to challenge, and expanded coverage is not the only or even the most powerful tool to improve population health. More than 400,000 Americans die every year from tobacco use, for example. A stiff increase in cigarette taxes (with the proceeds used to finance other needed tobacco control measures) would probably prevent more deaths than universal health coverage would.

We spend $2.3 trillion on medical care. Yet the public health system remains starved of vital resources for HIV [human immunodeficiency virus] prevention, reproductive health services, substance abuse prevention and treatment, and more. The Senate and House health reform bills both included important new public health funds to redress this imbalance. Whether these provisions will survive remains uncertain.

More generally, our society shows a tenuous commitment to investments outside medical care that profoundly affect population health. In the conclusion to our book, Robert Schoeni, George Kaplan, James House, and I note that America quietly lowers our sights in nearly every arena outside the domain of health. For example, Great Britain reduced child poverty by more than half through policies our own nation could replicate for perhaps $100 billion annually. The health benefits of such investments are hard to judge, but would probably be quite substantial.

A stiff increase in cigarette taxes . . . would probably prevent more deaths than universal health coverage would.

Of course, an 11-figure increase in income assistance, child care, and other redistributive programs seems politically impossible. Yet our annual *increase* in national health expenditures regularly exceeds this figure, seemingly on autopilot.

Ethicist Daniel Callahan muses that every American city includes gleaming hospitals and crumbling schools. That's not sustainable or wise, even if our only goal were to promote population health. For this reason and others, controlling the long-term growth of health care spending is essential. Health care spending is already crowding out other investments required to address critical national needs.

Nothing I just said provides a good argument against health reform. The economic and health benefits of near-universal coverage are quite large. No wealthy society should allow people to lose their homes because they get sick. Health reform would be a historic achievement. Still, it is only one step we must take to create a healthier and more decent society.

Chapter 3

Should the Purchase of Health Insurance Be Mandated by the Government?

Overview: How the Individual Mandate in the 2010 Health Reform Law Will Work

Alec MacGillis

Alec MacGillis is a staff writer at the Washington Post.

In a new book, *Landmark: The Inside Story of America's New Health Care Law and What It Means for Us All*, the staff of the *Washington Post* writes about various provisions of the new health law. Here is the chapter on mandatory insurance coverage.

A simple rule lies at the heart of the Patient Protection and Affordable Care Act: Starting in 2014, almost every American will need to carry health insurance or pay a fine. That rule is known as the individual mandate.

What It Means for You

The mandate requires all citizens and legal immigrants to have "qualifying" health coverage. People eligible for employer coverage can satisfy the requirement by enrolling in their employer's plan. Employer plans will need to meet certain standards—covering preventive care and disallowing lifetime limits—but will not need to have all of the minimum benefits that will be required of plans sold to individuals and small businesses.

People without insurance through their employer will be able to buy plans on new state-based insurance marketplaces called exchanges, where most will qualify for subsidies. The

Alec MacGillis, "Book Excerpt: How the Individual Health Insurance Mandate Will Work," *Kaiser Health News*, May 10, 2010. This information was reprinted with permission from the Henry J. Kaiser Family Foundation. The Kaiser Family Foundation is a non-profit private operating foundation, based in Menlo Park, California, dedicated to producing and communicating the best possible analysis and information on health issues.

lowest-price conventional insurance plan for sale on the exchanges must meet the minimum standard for qualifying health coverage: It must cover 60 percent of costs, and out-of-pocket expenses must be limited to $5,950 for individuals and $11,900 for families.

Starting in 2014, almost every American will need to carry health insurance or pay a fine.

There is an important exception: People younger than 30 will be able to satisfy the mandate by buying low-cost, high-deductible plans. The plans will require about $6,000 in out-of-pocket spending before most benefits kick in, though they will cover certain screening tests and immunizations before the deductible, and may cover some primary care visits as well. One advocacy group estimates that premiums for these plans will be $138 per month, compared with $190 per month for the least expensive conventional plan on the exchange. The thinking behind this option is that it will appeal to so-called young invincibles who believe they can do without broader coverage. Insurers argue, though, that if too many young people sign on to these plans, the risk pool in the conventional plans will be weighted too heavily toward older people.

What Will Happen If I Choose Not to Obtain Coverage?

You will be assessed a tax penalty that is the greater of a flat sum or a percent of income: $95 or 1 percent of income in 2014, $325 or 2 percent of income in 2015, and then the penalty's full level in 2016, $695 or 2.5 percent of income. After 2016, the flat dollar amount increases by a cost-of-living adjustment.

For children, the per-person sum is half the adult one. The maximum family penalty is the greater of 2.5 percent of income or three times the per-adult penalty ($2,085 in 2016).

All penalties are capped at the cost of the lowest-priced conventional plan on the exchanges.

What If I Can't Afford Coverage?

Hardship exemptions will be granted for those who are truly unable to afford insurance even with the subsidies that will be available—those for whom the least expensive plan option in their area exceeds 8 percent of their income. People who qualify for the hardship exemption also will be allowed to buy the high-deductible plan through the exchanges, even if they are older than 30.

Are There Any Exemptions?

People who lack coverage for a short period—up to three months—will not have to pay a penalty.

Exemptions also will be granted to people who choose not to seek medical care because of their religion, to Native Americans who are covered by the Indian Health Program, to veterans who are covered through the Department of Veterans Affairs, and to people in jail or prison.

Hardship exemptions will be granted for those who are truly unable to afford insurance even with the subsidies that will be available.

Illegal immigrants will not be subject to the mandate, nor will they be allowed to buy insurance through the exchanges. They will instead have to purchase coverage from companies that are still selling plans outside the exchanges, where government regulations and consumer protections will be lighter. They will be able to seek care, as they do now, at federally funded community health clinics and in hospital emergency rooms.

Hospitals that treat large numbers of poor patients will receive less federal support than they do now, on the rationale that more of their patients will be covered. But they will still get some aid in recognition of the fact that many immigrants will remain uncovered, and that some of their other patients will, at least at the outset, not obtain coverage. Whether that aid proves adequate remains to be seen—particularly in states such as California and Texas, where as many as 25 percent of residents are uninsured and there are high numbers of illegal immigrants.

What Will Happen If I Do Not Obtain Coverage or Pay the Fine?

Some opponents of the legislation conjured images of the government rounding up people and sending them to jail. But the law expressly states that failure to pay the penalties will not result in criminal prosecution or even in property liens. Also, the government probably will enforce the mandate loosely because of the political sensitivity of the health care law. In fact, those who wrote the legislation set the penalty for not carrying health coverage lower than what many health care experts believe is necessary for the mandate to work, precisely because they were worried about the political fallout from making the requirement seem too onerous.

Will It Work?

The relatively small penalty and the prospect of loose enforcement create a big potential problem: If many younger and healthier people decide to pay the fine instead of buying coverage, rates will increase for those who do buy it.

Some health care experts argue that the government will need to adopt a different approach. One option: Encourage everyone to obtain insurance but present those who do not with a choice. They could pay a much larger penalty than the one in the new law, while still retaining the ability to seek subsidized coverage if they do become sick; or they could sign a form on their tax return acknowledging that they were not insured and would therefore be ineligible for a fixed period—say, five years—for federal subsidies or for the protections in the law that allow people to buy coverage even if they have preexisting conditions. This would leave them facing a market with all the uncertainties of the current one. But creating an opt-out of this sort would address critics' concerns about the propriety or political risk of requiring people to have insurance.

The Massachusetts Experiment

Some of the law's supporters take heart in Massachusetts's experience with the individual mandate. Since that state adopted universal coverage in 2006, it has managed to get all but about 3 percent of its population insured. But Massachusetts started with a much higher percentage of the population covered than the rest of the country—9 percent of its residents were uninsured in 2006, compared with 15 percent in the entire United States now.

If many younger and healthier people decide to pay the fine instead of buying coverage, rates will increase for those who do buy it.

How did Massachusetts get to 97 percent coverage? The state government—working with hospitals, insurers and community groups—began an aggressive campaign to inform the public about the mandate and encourage compliance. The goal was to get people to think of having health insurance as a social norm, not unlike wearing a seat belt—something they would do because it was right and expected, regardless of the penalty for noncompliance.

The state made it easy to sign up: People who qualified for subsidized coverage received help filling out forms at hospitals and clinics, while others could use a website to determine whether they qualified for subsidies or could telephone the Health Connector, the state's version of the exchanges in the new federal law.

Residents were deluged with publicity. The Boston Red Sox promoted the mandate, pharmacy loudspeakers intoned it, grocery store receipts carried reminders and churches coaxed congregants. The Health Connector held 200 meetings with employers and two dozen outreach sessions; community groups received funding to help people sign up; and residents received red-lettered postcards in the mail.

It worked. A Health Connector board member said that a typical comment from young adults coming to apply for coverage was: "My mom said I had to sign up for health insurance or I would get into trouble."

But Jon Kingsdale, the program's executive director, says he worries about the prospects for duplicating the state's success nationally.

He thinks the penalty in the federal law is insufficient—in Massachusetts, the fine started at $219 and rose above $1,000 in 2010.

In addition, Massachusetts residents are accustomed to an activist state government, and the mandate was part of a law that had bipartisan support. It was signed by a Republican governor, Mitt Romney, who wrote in 2006: "Some of my libertarian friends balk at what looks like an individual mandate. But remember, someone has to pay for the health care that must, by law, be provided: Either the individual pays or the taxpayers pay. A free ride on the government is not libertarian."

Political Challenges

The national mandate will be implemented in a far more toxic political environment, making it more difficult for the government to create a nationwide expectation of compliance. The administration plans to start a promotional campaign as 2014 nears, much as [former president] George W. Bush's administration promoted the new Medicare drug benefit.

Within weeks of the signing, several legal challenges were already in the works from state attorneys general arguing that it is unconstitutional to require people to buy a given product, in this case health insurance. Most constitutional law experts, including those with conservative leanings, say that the mandate is constitutional, falling under the powers granted the federal government to impose taxes and to regulate interstate commerce.

Whatever the lawsuits' outcome, the momentum behind them suggests that come 2014, regardless of whether Democrats hold on to the White House, there will be deep pockets of resistance to the mandate. This could seriously complicate the implementation of a health care program that relies so much on the premise that everyone obtain coverage.

Americans Should Support the Individual Insurance Mandate Because It Is Necessary to Make Health Reform Work

Jonathan Cohn

Jonathan Cohn is a senior editor of the New Republic *magazine and author of the book* Sick: The Untold Story of America's Health Care Crisis—and the People Who Pay the Price.

Imagine for a moment that you work in a hospital emergency room. And just outside the door, a man has collapsed from a heart attack. Inside the facility, literally feet away from where he lies, are the equipment and knowledge to save his life. But this man doesn't have health insurance.

Would you treat him anyway? Or let him die?

If you think the way the vast majority of Americans do, you'd choose to save the man. Whatever your political attitudes, the thought of withholding lifesaving treatment from somebody because of ability to pay seems too cruel.

And that's fine. I'd make the same decision! But if you believe that, then you should also support what remains one of the most controversial elements of health care reform, even after its enactment. That element is the individual mandate.

Individual Mandate Is Necessary to Health Reform

An individual mandate is a requirement that everybody carry health insurance. Such requirements are a feature of every universal health care system in the world. And, under the recently passed Patient Protection and Affordable Care Act, they'd be a feature of America's health care system as well. Starting in 2014, Americans who don't obtain coverage either through a government program, through an employer-sponsored private policy or through a plan purchased directly through the new insurance exchanges would be subject to financial penalties.

Back in 2007 and early 2008, during the campaign for the Democratic presidential nomination, the mandate became a focus of dispute between the two front-runners, Hillary Clinton and Barack Obama. Clinton supported the mandate while Obama opposed it. But after becoming president and consulting with his advisers over how best to design a plan, Obama changed his mind and indicated he would support the idea.

A major goal of health reform is to make sure everybody . . . can get coverage.

Obama would end up arguing for the mandate largely on the same grounds that Clinton had: It was necessary, he said, in order for the rest of the insurance system to work. A major goal of health reform is to make sure everybody, even people with preexisting medical conditions, can get coverage. To accomplish that, you have to require that insurers offer policies to everybody, without discriminating against them based on health status. But imposing such a requirement would allow people to game the system: They could wait until they get sick and then buy coverage. The only way to avoid this problem is to make everybody carry insurance, even when they are healthy.

It's a technical argument more than a moral one. And it happens to be correct. For proof, one need look only at states that have imposed community rating (the requirement that insurers charge the same rates to people in different health conditions) and/or guaranteed issue (the requirement that insurers give policies even to people with medical problems) without a mandate. The requirements have made coverage more available to people in poor health, but only by raising premiums substantially, as insurers anticipate healthy people will opt out of coverage until they need it.

More Reasons to Support the Individual Mandate

Still, there are other reasons to support a mandate. One is explicitly about redistribution—from the medically lucky to the medically unlucky. At any one time, only a very small percentage of the population will have major health problems. The rough rule of thumb is that 20 percent of the people are responsible for about 80 percent of the costs in the system. But fortune (and misfortune) plays a huge role in determining who ends up as part of that 20 percent—all it takes is contracting a serious disease, having a debilitating accident or developing an acute condition. Rather than force this unlucky 20 percent to bear the burden of their medical expenses alone, you can ask everybody else—the people lucky enough to be in good health—to help shoulder that burden.

When you phrase it that way, the argument for a mandate sounds awfully liberal. But there is a third argument for the mandate—related, but from a different philosophical point of view. That's where the dying man outside the emergency room comes in.

The fact is that, even before the Affordable Care Act passed, the U.S. guaranteed health care in life-threatening situations. Under the Emergency Medical Treatment and Active Labor Act, which the Democratic Congress passed and President Ronald Reagan signed in 1986, providers of medical care must give stabilizing care to people who need it, regardless of ability to pay.

The law is hardly a substitute for universal coverage: It doesn't require that providers offer preventive or follow-up treatment and it allows them to collect huge bills afterwards.

But, in practice, many doctors and hospitals will end up providing quite a lot of charity care. And while they can pay for at least some of that out of their own revenues, they inevitably pass a portion of those bills onto everybody else, in the form of higher insurance premiums and higher taxes.

There are other reasons to support a mandate. One is explicitly about redistribution—from the medically lucky to the medically unlucky.

But some uninsured people who end up getting charity care could afford to pay for insurance premiums—or, at least, pay some portion of them. It might not be enough to offset the entire cost, but it'd be enough that they were making a reasonable contribution to the cost of their own care. And there's no reason they shouldn't. As one mandate supporter explained a few years ago, "for people who can afford to buy insurance, it's time for them to step up to the plate and buy that insurance."

Does that sound like a conservative argument? That's because it is. The quote is from a FOX News interview with former Massachusetts governor Mitt Romney, in 2006, not long after he signed into law that state's universal coverage scheme. Romney, of course, is a Republican. The Massachusetts system closely resembles the one the U.S. will get under the Affordable Care Act, complete with an individual mandate.

Today, Romney denounces the Affordable Care Act as an unconscionable government takeover of health care. And he is just one of many conservatives who supported the individual mandate before it became part of "Obamacare." But don't be fooled. If Romney and fellow Republicans weren't so determined to tarnish the Affordable Care Act politically, they'd acknowledge what they said before: The individual mandate makes perfect sense.

The Individual Insurance Mandate in Health Reform Is Not Unprecedented in American History

Maggie Mahar

Maggie Mahar is the health care fellow at the Century Foundation, a policy research institution. She is the author of the book Money-Driven Medicine: The Real Reason Health Care Costs So Much.

In "Bad Medicine," the [libertarian] Cato Institute white paper exploring "The Real Costs and Consequences of the New Health Care Law," Cato senior fellow Michael [D.] Tanner declares the individual mandate "perhaps the single most important piece of health care legislation." By insisting that citizens have insurance—or pay a penalty—Congress has taken an "unprecedented" step, says Tanner. Like many who object to the mandate, he argues that "the government has never required people to buy any good or service as a condition of lawful residence."

In fact, that isn't quite true.

But before getting to what the federal government has or hasn't required of its citizens in the past, let me say that I agree with Tanner on his first point: The individual mandate is the lynchpin at the center of the [Patient Protection and Affordable] Care Act (PPACA).

Why the Individual Mandate Is Central to Reform

Without the mandate, we could not require that insurers sell coverage to everyone, regardless of preexisting conditions. In

Maggie Mahar, "The Individual Mandate: A Reply to the Cato Institute's Report on Health Care Reform," *Taking Note* (blog), August 3, 2010. Reprinted by permission of Maggie Mahar, the Century Foundation.

the past, some insurers have refused to cover adults and children who are very sick. In other cases, they set the premiums so high that a middle-class person who had the bad luck to be struck down by a crippling disease could not afford the coverage. Sometimes insurers even canceled coverage if a customer became ill, arguing that he or she had concealed the disease when applying for the insurance.

Under the new law, insurers won't be allowed to shun the sick. They are required to cover anyone who applies for a policy, charging all customers in a given community the same price for the same coverage. (The only exception: Smokers and older customers will pay higher premiums.)

But what does this have to do with the mandate? If the law didn't insist that everyone have "minimal coverage" (or pay a financial penalty), many young, healthy Americans might well wait until they were injured, or seriously ill, before signing up for a policy—safe in the knowledge that no insurer could refuse them, or charge an exorbitant premium. If that happened, insurers would find themselves covering a pool made up largely of the elderly, the disabled, and the chronically ill. Premiums would skyrocket.

The individual mandate is the lynchpin at the center of the [Patient Protection and Affordable] Care Act (PPACA).

If we are going to try to provide health insurance for all citizens, the healthy must join the pool—or pay a penalty that will help defray the cost of covering everyone else. Recently, when I was speaking at a conference, a medical student asked me: "Why should a healthy person help pay for someone who is sick?" I replied, "There but for fortune. . . ." He nodded, and seemed satisfied.

The very idea of health insurance is predicated on the notion that none of us knows who will be laid low by accident or disease and when. The great advantage of insurance is that it spreads the risk over a large group of people exposed to the contingencies of fate. It is worth remembering that most disease and injuries can be traced to the accidents of one's gene pool (accounting for 30% of premature deaths), social circumstances (15%), "environmental factors" (such as air quality where you happened to grow up) (5%), or being in the wrong place at the wrong time, whether on the highway, playing a sport, riding a horse, or crossing a street.

By paying premiums, we also "pre-pay" for the routine care that we all need. This, too, serves a larger social good. If we ensure that everyone has access to preventive care, with no co-pays (something the new law guarantees), it is less likely that someone will need long-term acute care at some point in the future—treatment that the rest of us would wind up funding through taxes, higher insurance premiums or higher hospital fees.

But while Tanner and I agree that the mandate is central to the legislation, he does not share my view that it is essential because we hope to approach universal coverage. While discussing the individual mandate, Tanner never mentions that it is a prerequisite for covering everyone. By his lights, universal coverage doesn't appear to be a major goal. (Later in the report, Tanner explains that it just isn't doable. Under reform, he contends, insurers will continue to "cherry-pick" healthy patients by "locat[ing] their offices on the top floor of a building with no elevator; or provid[ing] free health club memberships while failing to include any oncologists in their network."

From Tanner's point of view, the mandate lies at the heart of the legislation because it is one way that the new law "rewrites the relationship between the government and the people," while raising "serious constitutional questions."

Is the Mandate Unprecedented?

This brings me to the argument that the attorneys general of some nineteen states are making, as they file challenges to the Patient Protection and Affordable Care Act, while making the constitutionality of the mandate a key issue in every case. Many agree with Tanner that the mandate is "unprecedented": *"The government has never required people to buy any good or service as a condition of lawful residence."*

In fact, that is precisely what Congress did, back in 1792.

The Original "Individual Mandate," Signed by President George Washington

In a provocative piece of legal research titled: "The Original Individual Mandate, Circa 1792," and published less than two weeks ago on [the website] Health Reform Watch, Seton Hall Law School's Bradley Latino explains: "The Militia Act of 1792, passed by the Second Congress and signed into law by President Washington, required every able-bodied white male citizen to enroll in his state's militia and mandated that he 'provide himself' with various goods for the common weal:

"'[E]ach and every free able-bodied white male citizen of the respective States . . . shall severally and respectively be enrolled in the militia . . . provid[ing] himself with a good musket or firelock, a sufficient bayonet and belt, two spare flints, and a knapsack, a pouch, with a box therein . . . and shall appear so armed, accoutred and provided, when called out to exercise or into service.'"

"This was the law of the land until the establishment of the National Guard in 1903," Latino explains. "For many American families, compliance meant purchasing—and eventually repurchasing—multiple muskets from a private party. Being required to purchase a musket was "no small thing," Latino continues. "Although anywhere from 40 to 79% of American households owned a firearm of some kind, the Militia Act specifically required a military-grade musket. That particular kind of gun was useful for traditional, line-up-and-shoot 18th-century warfare, but clumsy and inaccurate compared to the single-barrel shotguns and rifles Americans were using to hunt game. A new musket, alone, could cost anywhere from $250 to $500 in today's money. Some congressmen estimated it would cost £20 to completely outfit a man for militia service—about $2,000 today.

"Perhaps the most surprising aspect of the militia mandate," he adds, "is how uncontroversial it was. For instance, although the recently ratified Bill of Rights was certainly fresh on Congress's mind, not one of militia reform's many opponents thought to argue the mandate was a government taking of property for public use. Nor did anyone argue it to be contrary to states' rights under the Tenth Amendment. Rather, the mandate was criticized as an unfair burden upon the poor, who were asked to pay the same amount to arm themselves as the rich." [Unlike the health reform law, the mandate did not offer subsidies, nor did it allow citizens to pay a penalty in lieu of buying a musket.]

[The history of the Militia Act of 1792] reminds us of the responsibility . . . to "protect oneself and one's neighbors," even if that means requiring us to purchase . . . an insurance policy.

"Indeed," Latino notes, "the Militia Act did nothing to defray costs, although a few years later Congress did appropriate funds to pay militia members for the use of their time and goods—in effect subsidizing the purchases." He adds: "In fact, in light of the Militia Act, the individual mandate to purchase goods or services to protect oneself and one's neighbors can readily be described as 'deeply rooted in the history and traditions of the United States. . . .' The debate needs to be altered to accommodate this history."

Latino then comes to the crux of his argument: "As I continue researching the Militia Act and the militia system, what surprises me most, and what seems most relevant to the current populist arguments against health care reform in general, is how invested Americans once were in the idea of personal sacrifice. My favorite quotation comes from James 'Left Eye' Jackson, an anti-federalist-leaning congressmen who was no friend of the Washington administration:

> "'Though it may prove burthensome to some individuals to be obliged to arm themselves, yet it would not be so considered when the advantages were justly estimated. . . . [A]s this nation is rising fast in manufactures, the arts and sciences, and from her fertile soil may expect great affluence, she ought to protect that and her liberties from within herself.'"

Unlike Latino, I am not a student of the law, nor am I a constitutional scholar. I have no idea whether the Militia Act would hold up as a precedent in court. But I do think that this is a wonderfully relevant piece of our cultural history. It reminds us of the responsibility that President Washington and other founders believed that we as citizens have, to "protect oneself and one's neighbors," even if that means requiring us to purchase the thing that will defend us—be it a musket, or an insurance policy. I would argue that leaving 32 million Americans uninsured "threatens" our economy and our society, just as surely as an attack from abroad. When many don't receive the care they need, productivity drops, resentments between the haves and the have-nots widen—and all of us are exposed to the risks associated with living in an unhealthy and divided population.

An Individual Insurance Requirement in Health Reform Will Be Constitutional

Erwin Chemerinsky

Erwin Chemerinsky is a dean and professor at the School of Law of the University of California, Irvine.

Those opposing health care reform are increasingly relying on an argument that has no legal merit: that the health care reform legislation would be unconstitutional. There is, of course, much to debate about how to best reform America's health care system. But there is no doubt that bills passed by House and Senate committees are constitutional.

Health Insurance Affects Interstate Commerce

Some who object to the health care proposals claim that they are beyond the scope of congressional powers. Specifically, they argue that Congress lacks the authority to compel people to purchase health insurance or pay a tax or a fine.

Congress clearly could do this under its power pursuant to Article I, Section 8 of the Constitution to regulate commerce among the states. The Supreme Court has held that this includes authority to regulate activities that have a substantial effect on interstate commerce. In the area of economic activities, "substantial effect" can be found based on the cumulative impact of the activity across the country. For example, a few years ago, the Supreme Court held that Congress could use its commerce clause authority to prohibit individuals from cultivating and possessing small amounts of marijuana for personal medicinal use because marijuana is bought and sold in interstate commerce.

Erwin Chemerinsky, "Health Care Reform Is Constitutional," *Politico*, October 23, 2009. Reprinted by permission.

The relationship between health care coverage and the national economy is even stronger and more readily apparent. In 2007, health care expenditures amounted to $2.2 trillion, or $7,421 per person, and accounted for 16.2 percent of the gross domestic product.

Ken Klukowski, writing in *Politico*, argued that "people who declined to purchase government-mandated insurance would not be engaging in commercial activity, so there's no interstate commerce." Klukowski's argument is flawed because the Supreme Court never has said that the commerce power is limited to regulating those who are engaged in commercial activity.

Quite the contrary: The court has said that Congress can use its commerce power to forbid hotels and restaurants from discriminating based on race, even though their conduct was refusing to engage in commercial activity. Likewise, the court has said that Congress can regulate the growing of marijuana for personal medicinal use, even if the person being punished never engaged in any commercial activity.

[There is no] basis for arguing that an insurance requirement violates individual liberties. No constitutionally protected freedom is infringed.

Under an unbroken line of precedents stretching back 70 years, Congress has the power to regulate activities that, taken cumulatively, have a substantial effect on interstate commerce. People not purchasing health insurance unquestionably has this effect.

There is a substantial likelihood that everyone will need medical care at some point. A person with a communicable disease will be treated whether or not he or she is insured. A person in an automobile accident will be rushed to the hospital for treatment, whether or not he or she is insured. Congress would simply be requiring everyone to be insured to cover their potential costs to the system.

An Exercise of Congress's Power to Tax and Spend

Congress also could justify this as an exercise of its taxing and spending power. Congress can require the purchase of health insurance and then tax those who do not do so in order to pay their costs to the system. This is similar to Social Security taxes, which everyone pays to cover the costs of the Social Security system. Since the 1930s, the Supreme Court has accorded Congress broad powers to tax and spend for the general welfare and has left it to Congress to determine this.

Nor is there any basis for arguing that an insurance requirement violates individual liberties. No constitutionally protected freedom is infringed. There is no right to not have insurance. Most states now require automobile insurance as a condition for driving.

Since the 19th century, the Supreme Court has consistently held that a tax cannot be challenged as an impermissible take of private property for public use without just compensation. All taxes are a taking of private property for public use, but no tax has ever been invalidated on that basis.

Since the late 1930s, the Supreme Court has ruled that government economic regulations, including taxes, are to be upheld as long as they are reasonable. Virtually all economic regulations and taxes have been found to meet this standard for more than 70 years. There is thus no realistic chance that the mandate for health insurance would be invalidated for denying due process or equal protection.

Those who object to the health care proposals on constitutional grounds are making an argument that has no basis in the law. They are invoking the rhetorical power of the Constitution to support their opposition to health care reform, but the law is clear that Congress constitutionally has the power to do so. There is much to argue about in the debate over health care reform, but constitutionality is not among the hard questions to consider.

The Individual Insurance Mandate in Health Reform Is Bad Public Policy

Jon Walker

Jon Walker is a frequent blogger at FDL Action, a site founded and published by Jane Hamsher, a writer, author, and film producer.

Since the big victory for Prop C [Proposition C, a measure to exempt Missouri residents from the individual insurance mandate in the 2010 health care law] in Missouri, I've seen several "progressives" rush to defend the individual mandate that requires individuals to buy private insurance. I find such action indefensible for individuals who call themselves progressives. At most, progressives should think of the individual mandate to buy poorly regulated private health insurance as a highly suboptimal solution to expanding coverage. The mandate is neither good politics nor good policy. Defending it strikes me as nothing more than a reflective defense of the Democratic Party masquerading as progressivism.

Alternatives to the Individual Mandate

If the true goal of progressives is to produce truly universal health insurance in the best, most cost-effective manner, then there is no honest progressive who would recommend the individual mandate. There must be at least a half dozen better policy solutions to the problem.

A universal single-payer health care system, such as Medicare for all, is probably as close as you can get to an optimal solution. It is dramatically better by all measures than a system based on an individual mandate.

Jon Walker, "Progressives Shouldn't Defend the Individual Mandate: The Difference Between Ideology and Blind Partisan Defense," FDL Action, August 6, 2010. Reproduced by permission.

Even if you wanted to keep a mainly private health insurance exchange system, there are several second-best options that are better policies than the government collecting an individual mandate tax. One option is creating an extremely bare-bones default public health insurance plan that would automatically cover anyone who didn't sign up for a private insurance plan.

Another option would be for the government to select the private plan from the lowest level with the best metrics and automatically enroll everyone without insurance in that plan. If their subsidies fully cover the cost, then there is no problem. If their subsidies are not enough, then additional money would be automatically withheld from their earnings along with their payroll taxes. Wealthier individuals would have the ability to opt out of this automatic withholding only if they sign away their right to community ratings and subsidies for a set time or accept that they will have to pay a large penalty if they sign up after getting ill.

[The individual mandate] is not the best solution, or even the second or third best solution, for expanding coverage.

Obviously, I feel that giving people the choice of a public option makes the individual mandate a noticeably worse policy. With the public option, the government is technically only requiring you to give money to a government agency instead of making it a crime not to hand money over to a private company.

I would even consider it a policy improvement to replace the government-run individual mandate with a premium back payment penalty that is combined with the government sending out directed warning letters. That gives insurance companies the right to charge people a back premium penalty worth up to six months of premiums if they try to sign up for insurance without being able to prove they were previously insured. It creates nearly the same type of financial incentive to not be a "free rider" (that is, wait until you get sick to sign up for insurance), without the creepy idea of the government actually forcing you to buy a product from a private company.

An Ugly Compromise

I accept that some progressives honestly feel the new system created by the law with the individual mandate is an improvement over the *status quo*, but no one should pretend that it is actually good policy rather than the ugly compromise that it really is. It is not the best solution, or even the second or third best solution, for expanding coverage. Progressives do themselves a huge disservice when they defend this piece of poor policy and bad politics. What they should be doing now is acknowledging that the individual mandate isn't good and needs to be replaced with a more progressive alternative.

I can only compare the individual mandate to "Don't Ask, Don't Tell" [a policy regarding homosexuals in the US military] back in the 90s. It was technically an improvement over the then *status quo*, but it was still an ugly, stupid policy. While possibly better than what was happening before, it was clearly a suboptimal solution. Just like "Don't Ask, Don't Tell," progressives should not pretend that the individual mandate is a good idea simply because it is part of the bad compromise created by "their" party. That is the difference between true ideological activists and people who see themselves as defenders of the party even when the party's ideas are truly bad.

There Are No Precedents for the Individual Insurance Mandate in the New Health Reform Law

Julia Shaw

Julia Shaw is a frequent blogger at The Foundry, *a blog published by the Heritage Foundation, a conservative think tank.*

As soon as President Barack Obama signed the [Patient Protection and Affordable Care Act] of 2010 into law, Virginia Attorney General Ken Cuccinelli filed suit against the federal government, arguing that the legislation is unconstitutional.

Cuccinelli highlights the individual mandate as particularly offensive to the Constitution, emphasizing that "at no time in our history has the government mandated its citizens buy a good or service."

Some disagree with Cuccinelli, pointing to the second Militia Act of 1792 as evidence that the individual mandate is not unprecedented and furthermore that the founders would have supported the recent health care bill. This argument is analytically defective. The second Militia Act of 1792 neither sanctions nor foreshadows the individual mandate in the recently passed health care legislation.

The Individual Mandate Is Broader in Scope

Some point to this list of requirements in the second Militia Act as evidence that Congress has, in fact, required its citizens to purchase a good or service. The second Militia Act of 1792

Julia Shaw, "The Use and Abuse of the Founders: The Individual Mandate Is Still Unprecedented and Unconstitutional," *The Foundry* (blog), March 26, 2010. Reprinted by permission.

indeed states "that every citizen, so enrolled and notified, shall, within six months thereafter, provide himself with a good musket or firelock, a sufficient bayonet and belt, two spare flints, and a knapsack, a pouch, with a box therein, to contain not less than twenty-four cartridges, suited to the bore of his musket or firelock, each cartridge to contain a proper quantity of powder and ball; or with a good rifle, knapsack, shot-pouch, and powder horn, twenty balls suited to the bore of his rifle, and a quarter of a pound of powder." Since the Second Congress passed the second Militia Act that requires members of the militia to procure a musket and bullets, it is therefore suggested that the founders (and the Constitution) would also have supported the recent health care bill that requires all members of society to purchase health insurance. Support of the second Militia Act does not imply support for the health care bill.

The second Militia Act of 1792 neither sanctions nor foreshadows the individual mandate in the recently passed health care legislation.

Unlike the reach of the health care bill, the second Militia Act applies to a narrow subsection of society: white, male citizens between the ages of eighteen and forty-five who are members of the militia. Section I of the act, which includes the list of required goods, begins: "Be it enacted by the Senate and House of Representatives of the United States of America, in Congress assembled, That each and every free able-bodied white male citizen of the respective States, resident therein, who is or shall be of age of eighteen years, and under the age of forty-five years (except as is herein after excepted) shall severally and respectively be enrolled in the militia." It follows that the second Militia Act would not apply to anyone not enrolled in the militia: including noncitizens, the infirm, men younger than eighteen, men older than forty-five, or women.

Section II of the act further exempts a whole host of men, despite fitting the age and fitness requirements, from participating in the militia and therefore the requirement of procuring muskets, bullets, and other such items pertaining to militia service. Specifically exempted from the militia are the vice president of the United States, judicial and executive officers, members of the House and Senate, post officers, certain ferry officers and stage drivers to name a few. Moreover, the language of the statute requires a member of the militia to "provide himself" with the list of goods. It is possible that a man could have inherited a musket, bartered for a knapsack, or made his own bullets, and still be in compliance with the act. In contrast to the second Militia Act, the health care bill applies to any living breathing person in America to purchase health insurance. It is unlikely one could inherit, barter, or create one's own health insurance and avoid the penalty of the law.

The Lack of a Constitutional Basis

The greatest difference between the health care bill and the second Militia Act is constitutionality. There is solid constitutional basis for the second Militia Act: Article I, Section 8, Clause 16 states that Congress has the power "to provide for organizing, arming, and disciplining the Militia, and for governing such Part of them as may be employed in the Service of the United States, reserving to the States respectively, the Appointment of the Officers, and the Authority of training the Militia according to the discipline prescribed by Congress." Articulating a list of goods required for militia service is certainly within the bounds of this clause. Indeed, "Federalist [No.] 29" emphasizes that such regulation of the militia is part of "superintending the common defense, and of watching over the internal peace of the Confederacy."

In contrast to the second Militia Act, the health care legislation lacks any constitutional basis or legal precedent to support its requirement that every living person in America purchase health care insurance. Some have suggested the Commerce Clause to be the basis for the individual mandate. But this is wrong. The Commerce Clause does not empower Congress to impose a duty on individuals as members of society to purchase a specific service that would be heavily regulated by the federal government. To be clear, neither the original meaning of the clause nor even the most expansive court interpretation of the Commerce Clause authorized the individual mandate.

The individual mandate is deeply problematic and truly unprecedented. While it is important to look to founders' writings and examples to guide today's policy questions, one should avoid selectively quoting and ultimately mischaracterizing the founders.

The Supreme Court Is Likely to Find the Individual Insurance Mandate Unconstitutional

Randy Barnett

Randy Barnett is a senior fellow at the libertarian Cato Institute, a professor of constitutional law at Georgetown University, and the author of the book Restoring the Lost Constitution: The Presumption of Liberty.

A "tell" in poker is a subtle but detectable change in a player's behavior or demeanor that reveals clues about the player's assessment of his hand. Something similar has happened with regard to the insurance mandate at the core of last month's [March 2010's] health reform legislation. Congress justified its authority to enact the mandate on the grounds that it is a regulation of commerce. But as this justification came under heavy constitutional fire, the mandate's defenders changed the argument—now claiming constitutional authority under Congress's power to tax.

This switch in constitutional theories is a tell: Defenders of the bill lack confidence in their commerce power theory. The switch also comes too late. When the mandate's constitutionality comes up for review as part of the state attorneys general lawsuit, the Supreme Court will not consider the penalty enforcing the mandate to be a tax because, in the provision that actually defines and imposes the mandate and penalty, Congress did not call it a tax and did not treat it as a tax.

Randy Barnett, "The Insurance Mandate in Peril," Cato Institute, April 29, 2010. Reprinted from The Wall Street Journal © 2010, Dow Jones & Company. All rights reserved.

Problems with the Commerce Clause Argument

The Patient Protection and Affordable Care Act (aka ObamaCare) includes what it calls an "individual responsibility requirement" that all persons buy health insurance from a private company. Congress justified this mandate under its power to regulate commerce among the several states: "The individual responsibility requirement provided for in this section," the law says, ". . . is commercial and economic in nature, and substantially affects interstate commerce, as a result of the effects described in paragraph (2)." Paragraph (2) then begins: "The requirement regulates activity that is commercial and economic in nature: economic and financial decisions about how and when health care is paid for, and when health insurance is purchased."

In this way, the statute speciously tries to convert inactivity into the "activity" of making a "decision." By this reasoning, your "decision" not to take a job, not to sell your house, or not to buy a Chevrolet is an "activity that is commercial and economic in nature" that can be mandated by Congress.

Defenders of the bill lack confidence in their commerce power theory.

It is true that the Supreme Court has interpreted the Commerce Clause broadly enough to reach wholly intrastate economic "activity" that substantially affects interstate commerce. But the Court has never upheld a requirement that individuals who are doing nothing must engage in economic activity by entering into a contractual relationship with a private company. Such a claim of power is literally unprecedented.

Problems with the Tax Argument

Since this Commerce Clause language was first proposed in the Senate last December [2009], Democratic legislators and law professors alike breezily dismissed any constitutional objections as preposterous. After the bill was enacted, critics branded lawsuits by state attorneys general challenging the insurance mandate as frivolous. Yet, unable to produce a single example of Congress using its commerce power this way, the defenders of the personal mandate began to shift grounds.

On March 21 [2010], the same day the House approved the Senate version of the legislation, the staff of the Joint Committee on Taxation released a 157-page "technical explanation" of the bill. The word "commerce" appeared nowhere. Instead, the personal mandate is dubbed an "Excise Tax on Individuals Without Essential Health Benefits Coverage." But while the enacted bill does impose excise taxes on "high-cost," employer-sponsored insurance plans and "indoor tanning services," the statute never describes the regulatory "penalty" it imposes for violating the mandate as an "excise tax." It is expressly called a "penalty."

This shift won't work. The Supreme Court will not allow staffers and lawyers to change the statutory cards that Congress already dealt when it adopted the Senate language.

In the 1920s, when Congress wanted to prohibit activity that was then deemed to be solely within the police power of states, it tried to penalize the activity using its tax power. In *Bailey v. Drexel Furniture Co.* (1922) the Supreme Court struck down such a penalty saying, "there comes a time in the extension of the penalizing features of the so-called tax when it loses its character as such and becomes a mere penalty with the characteristics of regulation and punishment."

Although the Court has never repudiated this principle, the Court now interprets the commerce power far more broadly. Thus Congress may regulate or prohibit intrastate economic activity directly without invoking its taxation power. Yet precisely because a mandate to engage in economic activity has never been upheld by the Court, the tax power is once again being used to escape constitutional limits on Congress's regulatory power.

Supporters of the mandate cite *U.S. v. Kahriger* (1953), where the Court upheld a punitive tax on gambling by saying that "[u]nless there are provisions extraneous to any tax need, courts are without authority to limit the exercise of the taxing power." Yet the Court in *Kahriger* also cited *Bailey* with approval. The key to understanding *Kahriger* is the proposition the Court there rejected: "It is said that Congress, under the pretense of exercising its power to tax, has attempted to penalize illegal intrastate gambling through the regulatory features of the Act" (emphasis added).

In other words, the Court in *Kahriger* declined to look behind Congress's assertion that it was exercising its tax power to see whether a measure was really a regulatory penalty. As the Court said in *Sonzinsky v. U.S.* (1937), "[i]nquiry into the hidden motives which may move Congress to exercise a power constitutionally conferred upon it is beyond the competency of courts." But this principle cuts both ways. Neither will the Court look behind Congress's inadequate assertion of its commerce power to speculate as to whether a measure was "really" a tax. The Court will read the cards as Congress dealt them.

Because a mandate to engage in economic activity has never been upheld by the Court, the tax power is . . . being used to escape constitutional limits on Congress's regulatory power.

Congress simply did not enact the personal insurance mandate pursuant to its tax powers. To the contrary, the statute expressly says the mandate "regulates activity that is commercial and economic in nature." It never mentions the tax power and none of its eight findings mention raising any revenue with the penalty.

Moreover, while inserting the mandate into the Internal Revenue Code, Congress then expressly severed the penalty from the normal enforcement mechanisms of the tax code.

The failure to pay the penalty "shall not be subject to any criminal prosecution or penalty with respect to such failure." Nor shall the IRS [Internal Revenue Service] "file notice of lien with respect to any property of a taxpayer by reason of any failure to pay the penalty imposed by this section," or "levy on any such property with respect to such failure."

In short, the "penalty" is explicitly justified as a penalty to enforce a regulation of economic activity and not as a tax. There is no authority for the Court to recharacterize a regulation as a tax when doing so is contrary to the express and actual regulatory purpose of Congress.

So defenders of the mandate are making yet another unprecedented claim. Never before has the Court looked behind Congress's unconstitutional assertion of its commerce power to see if a measure could have been justified as a tax. For that matter, never before has a "tax" penalty been used to mandate, rather than discourage or prohibit, economic activity.

Are there now five justices willing to expand the commerce and tax powers of Congress where they have never gone before? Will the Court empower Congress to mandate any activity on the theory that a "decision" not to act somehow affects interstate commerce? Will the Court accept that Congress has the power to mandate any activity so long as it is included in the Internal Revenue Code and the IRS does the enforcing?

Yes, the smart money is always on the Court upholding an act of Congress. But given the hand Congress is now holding, I would not bet the farm.

CHAPTER 4

Will the PPACA Improve Medical Care for the Uninsured?

Chapter Preface

In March 2010, the US Congress enacted the Patient Protection and Affordable Care Act (PPACA)—a package of health care reforms championed by President Barack Obama. Although the process of passing the legislation was extremely contentious, the result was historic—universal health care for almost all Americans, achieved through mandates on both employers and individuals, with government subsidies to make health insurance affordable. The new law also targets a number of insurance abuses, contains cost-cutting changes for Medicare, and includes a number of demonstration and pilot projects to test ways of improving the health care system. The law is highly complex, but some of its major provisions are described below.

The PPACA's biggest changes are postponed until 2014, but several fairly significant changes are made in the very first year. For example, the PPACA in 2010 requires that children with preexisting conditions be covered and that dependent children under the age of twenty-six be allowed to remain on their parents' health insurance policies. Also in 2010, insurance companies are prohibited from rescinding health insurance once subscribers become ill and prevented from imposing lifetime or unreasonable yearly limits on benefits. The PPACA further requires insurers to implement a new appeals process and provide coverage for preventive services without co-pays. However, certain reforms, such as those requiring coverage of preventive care, will not be applied to grandfathered plans—defined as plans in existence as of March 2010 when the PPACA was enacted.

Also beginning in 2010, persons with preexisting medical conditions can apply for coverage through a federal high-risk insurance pool. In addition, the act requires a $250 rebate in 2010 to seniors to help them pay for prescription drugs not covered by Medicare; this gap in Medicare's prescription coverage, often referred to as the "doughnut hole," will be completely closed by 2020. Other early changes include a 10 percent tax on indoor tanning services, and tax credits for businesses with fewer than fifty employees to cover 35 percent of their health care premiums (increasing to 50 percent by 2014).

In 2011, the PPACA requires insurers to spend at least 80–85 percent of premium dollars on direct medical care and efforts to improve the quality of care. A number of other 2011 changes will affect Medicare. For example, two important changes are that Medicare will be required to cover annual wellness visits and personalized prevention plans and that a 50 percent discount will be provided on brand-name drugs for seniors. In addition, the Medicare payroll tax will increase from 1.45 percent to 2.35 percent for individuals earning more than $200,000 (and married couples filing jointly earning above $250,000). The changes scheduled for 2012 and 2013 are mostly administrative. For example, in 2012 the law requires health insurers to begin implementing standards for the electronic exchange of health information in order to reduce paperwork and administrative costs.

The most significant changes occur in 2014. At that time, insurance companies will no longer be allowed to deny coverage to adults with preexisting health conditions, and insurers will be prohibited from denying coverage or setting rates based on gender, health status, medical condition, claims experience, genetic information, evidence of domestic violence, or other health-related factors. In addition, employer and individual mandates kick in during 2014. Businesses with fifty or more employees will be required to offer coverage to employees or pay a $2,000 penalty per employee. Individuals who are not covered by their employers will be required to purchase basic health insurance or pay a fine ($95 in 2014, $325 in 2015, $695 or up to 2.5 percent of income in 2016).

However, there is government help for poor and middle-class Americans who may find it difficult to purchase insurance. First, Medicaid will be expanded in 2014 to completely cover people whose income is up to 133 percent of the poverty level. Also, the PPACA will allow exceptions from the individual mandate for financial hardship. In addition, the PPACA will provide subsidies to help people purchase insurance. These subsidies will be in the form of refundable tax credits and will be available for Americans with incomes between 100 and 400 percent of the federal poverty line, or about $88,000 for a family of four. Finally, in 2014 the act requires states to contract with private insurers to create multistate health insurance exchanges to help individuals and small employers shop for affordable plans. Plans offered on these new exchanges must provide essential health benefits and are restricted in various ways: They cannot require deductibles higher than $2,000 for individuals and $4,000 for families; they cannot require excessive out-of-pocket payments; and coverage must be offered at four levels—90 percent, 80 percent, 70 percent, and 60 percent.

The PPACA reforms are paid for by changes in Medicare and by a tax that will take effect in 2018 on so-called Cadillac plans—health insurance plans of more than $27,500 for family coverage and $10,200 for single coverage. Also, the government will impose new fees on drug manufacturers, health insurance companies, and medical device manufacturers.

The Congressional Budget Office (CBO) estimates that the PPACA will provide health coverage to an additional 32 million currently uninsured Americans, and many health care experts hope the law's many reforms will lead to a better US health care system for all Americans. Opponents, however, have promised to fight the PPACA's implementation, claiming it will leave millions still uninsured, that it will involve the government too much in health care, and that it will only increase health care costs for everyone. The authors of the viewpoints in this chapter debate whether the PPACA will improve medical care for the millions of people currently uninsured.

The Health Care Reform Law Creates Tremendous Opportunities to Improve the Quality of US Health Care

Mark B. McClellan

Mark B. McClellan is the director of the Engelberg Center for Health Care Reform, a project of the Brookings Institution, a public policy organization.

The passage of comprehensive health care reform legislation presents tremendous opportunities to improve the way that America's health care system works. Reforms to expand coverage hold the potential to help millions of Americans. But in order to sustain this coverage and assure it provides access to innovative care, we need to focus on helping all Americans get the best care, not just better coverage.

While the new law will result in many more Americans having access to health insurance, changes in insurance coverage alone won't ensure that they receive high-quality, innovative health care. Instead, how health care reform legislation is implemented will be critical to this effort.

Focusing on Quality

Currently, information on the quality and cost of health care is woefully inadequate. However, a number of provisions in the law provide a stronger foundation for addressing quality of care—establishing broad national priorities for quality improvement and taking steps toward implementing nationally consistent performance measures that focus on outcomes, patient experience, and other aspects of care that really matter to

Mark B. McClellan, "Better Health Care at Lower Costs: Real Health Care Reform," Brookings Institution, April 15, 2010. Reprinted by permission.

patients. Having such information about the performance of doctors, hospitals, and other health care providers can provide a trusted basis for changing payments, benefits, and other health care policies. But it's not just about measuring cost and quality of care; we must also take feasible steps to act on those measures and improve care.

Paying for Better Care, Not More Care

Some of the most important payment system reforms are those that pay doctors and hospitals more when they get better health outcomes at an overall lower cost—and that make it easier for doctors and patients to change the way that health care works to make that happen. Many ideas have been proposed to improve how doctors could work together to reduce complications of diabetes and other chronic diseases, such as by using electronic medical records or working with nurse practitioners who can help patients use their prescription drugs more effectively. The most important reforms on the payment side don't tell doctors and hospitals what they need to do but support them when they figure out how to do things better.

Supporting Improvements with Better Evidence

Provider payment reforms included in the law represent—as the president likes to say—a lot of the ideas that experts have put forth. The challenge is that we don't really know which of these will actually work best, so we'll have to find out quickly which of those reforms really work to improve care and lower costs. This will require doing a fundamentally better job of running the pilot and demonstration programs in Medicare. Typically, these can take eight to 10 years to test and evaluate proposed reforms—and we don't have that kind of time to reduce spending growth.

Indeed, more and better information that's more readily available is needed to support wide-ranging improvements not only in the quality and value of care, but across the health care system. This data can do important things to improve quality and payment system reforms, but can also support other needed changes, such as improvements in medical product safety.

Some of the most important payment system reforms are those that pay doctors and hospitals more when they get better health outcomes at an overall lower cost.

Health care reform has been enacted, but the hard work is far from over. Much more can and must be done to ensure that health care in the U.S. really does become a system of highly innovative care at lower costs for all Americans.

Uninsured Women Will Benefit Greatly from the PPACA's Reforms

Sara R. Collins, Sheila Rustgi, and Michelle M. Doty

Sara R. Collins is vice president of the Affordable Health Insurance program of the Commonwealth Fund, a private research organization focused on health care issues. Sheila Rustgi is a program associate for the project. Michelle M. Doty is assistant vice president and director of survey research for the Commonwealth Fund.

The [Patient Protection and] Affordable Care Act ([PP]ACA) is likely to stabilize and reverse women's growing exposure to health care costs over the next decade. Up to 15 million women who now are uninsured could gain subsidized coverage under the law. And 14.5 million "underinsured" women will benefit from provisions that improve coverage.

While women are as likely as men to be without health insurance, their role as caregivers and their own unique health care needs leave them more exposed to the rapidly rising costs of care and to the problems resulting from loss of health coverage. Because insurance carriers consider women, particularly young women, a higher risk than men, women experience more difficulty obtaining coverage from the individual market and are charged much higher premiums for the same benefits than men of the same age. Most policies sold in the individual market, moreover, will not cover the costs of a pregnancy. Women's higher health care costs mean that they are more likely than men to experience problems paying medical bills—their own and those of family members. And women, both in-

Sara R. Collins, Sheila Rustgi, and Michelle M. Doty, "How Women Will Benefit from the ACA," The Commonwealth Fund, July 30, 2010. Reprinted by permission.

sured and uninsured, are more likely than men to delay health care to avoid the associated costs.

While women and their families will realize the greatest benefits from the expansion and improvement of insurance coverage beginning in 2014, several [PP]ACA provisions that are to be implemented during 2010—or have already been implemented—will provide important transitional support. The provisions that will benefit women, and their expected impact, are summarized below.

Changes for 2010–2013

Requirement that employers and insurers allow adult children up to age 26 to join or remain on a parent's health plan (Sept. 2010). Nearly 1 million uninsured adult children are expected to gain coverage through their parents' policies over the next three years, while another 600,000 currently enrolled in individual market plans will gain more affordable coverage by joining their parents' plans.

Ban on lifetime coverage limits (Sept. 2010). About 102 million people have health plans with lifetime benefit limits, and each year up to 20,400 people exceed their plan limits and lose coverage. Assuming that women make up half the population, about 10,000 women would gain coverage as a result of the ban.

[Women's] role as caregivers and their own unique health care needs leave them more exposed to the rapidly rising costs of care.

Phased-in restrictions on annual benefit limits (Sept. 2010). An estimated 18 million people have health plans with annual benefit limits. The [Patient Protection and] Affordable Care Act increases the cap on annual limits over 2010–2013, before banning them completely in 2014. By 2013, up to 3,500 people will gain coverage as a result of the ban, about 1,750 of them women.

Bans on rescissions of coverage (Sept. 2010). About 15 million people who have coverage through the individual insurance market, where rescissions, or cancellations, of health policies are most common, will benefit from this ban. About 10,700 people, including 5,350 women, are estimated to have their coverage rescinded each year.

Preexisting condition insurance plans (July–Aug. 2010). An estimated 200,000 people, including approximately 100,000 women who have serious health problems and have had difficulty obtaining insurance coverage, will gain coverage through these plans over the next three years.

Rebates to Medicare beneficiaries in the drug coverage doughnut hole (2010). Each year, about 16 percent of Medicare beneficiaries—a disproportionate number of them women—will hit the "doughnut hole" in their prescription drug coverage. Starting this year, beneficiaries will receive $250 rebates when they reach the hole, which will be phased out completely by 2020.

Women and their families will realize the greatest benefits from the expansion and improvement of insurance coverage beginning in 2014.

Changes for 2014 and Beyond

Expansion in Medicaid eligibility to cover adults with incomes below 133 percent of the federal poverty level ($29,000 for a family of four) (Jan. 2014). The expansion in Medicaid has the potential to cover up to 8.2 million currently uninsured adult women under age 65.

New state health insurance exchanges with premium and cost-sharing subsidies for people with low and moderate incomes

(Jan. 2014). Uninsured women who earn too much to qualify for Medicaid will be able to purchase policies through state-run exchanges with those earning less than 400 percent of poverty ($88,000 for a family of four) eligible for subsidies to offset premiums and out-of-pocket costs. Up to 7 million uninsured adult women under age 65 may gain subsidized coverage through the exchanges.

Essential health benefit standards that include maternity care, as well as limits on cost sharing, for plans sold in insurance exchanges and in the individual and small-group markets (Jan. 2014). This provision will ensure that all women have health plans that cover the cost of a pregnancy, a major gap in the individual insurance market, where only 13 percent of health plans now include maternity benefits. The new benefit standard and out-of-pocket spending limits will help uninsured women who earn too much to qualify for Medicaid or premium subsidies gain comprehensive coverage and also promise to significantly reduce the estimated 14.5 million women who are considered underinsured because of their high out-of-pocket costs relative to income.

Prohibitions on insurance carriers from denying coverage or charging higher premiums on the basis of health or gender (Jan. 2014). An estimated 7.3 million women—38 percent—who tried to buy health insurance in the individual market over a recent three-year period were turned down, charged a higher premium, or had a condition excluded from coverage because it was preexisting. Moreover, rating on the basis of gender is currently permitted in the individual market in 42 states, while 38 states allow insurance carriers to take into account gender in pricing health insurance policies for small businesses, a blow to women in companies with predominantly female workforces. Millions of women will benefit from the new rules prohibiting denial of coverage or higher premiums based on health or gender.

Together, these provisions will ensure that women and their families can get the health care they need without the risk of incurring catastrophic medical bills.

Health Insurance for the Uninsured Will Improve Care for All Americans

Eric B. Larson

Eric B. Larson is executive director of the Group Health Research Institute, a public policy research organization within Group Health Cooperative, a health care system based in Seattle, Washington.

Perhaps your family earns enough to be called "rich" and to be taxed to help pay for expanding health care coverage to the uninsured under the U.S. House's new bill. Or more likely you're just lucky enough to get health coverage through your employer or are covered by Medicare.

Either way, you might feel removed from the estimated 47 million U.S. residents who lack health insurance. Sure, you may empathize with their plight: not quite poor enough for Medicaid or old enough for Medicare, and unable to afford their own insurance.

Still, you probably don't expect that covering the uninsured will help you out. But a recent report from the National Academy of Sciences' Institute of Medicine (IOM) suggests, surprisingly, that it will. The report, called "America's Uninsured Crisis[: Consequences for Health and Health Care]," concludes that the U.S. health-coverage crisis has dire consequences for all of us, including people with good health insurance and for health care providers too.

The Uninsured Crisis Harms Everyone's Health Care

"America's Uninsured Crisis" describes how high rates of "uninsurance" have harmed the health care that's available to

Eric B. Larson, "Health Insurance for Uninsured Will Improve Care for All Americans," *Seattle Times*, July 20, 2009. Reprinted by permission.

people with good health insurance. As more and more people in an area become uninsured, it leads to deterioration in community services like access to emergency rooms, primary medical care and certain specialists needed in emergencies. Such declines are now visible in many U.S. cities, towns and neighborhoods.

A recent study the IOM commissioned suggests that when uninsurance rates are high, it's harder for even insured adults to get the health care they need. And doctors, who are generally paid more for providing more tests and treatments, may be more likely to believe that they can't make clinical decisions in the patient's best interest without losing income. In response, even many public service institutions such as non-profit hospitals are preferentially building profitable "service lines," typically those involving highly rewarded surgical procedures and diagnostic tests that can be scheduled in advance. These service lines are usually built at the expense of more basic and valuable services like maternity care, trauma services and acute care.

Meanwhile, with its dwindling supply of general internists or family practice doctors, the nation's primary care system is on life support and in danger of dying altogether as graduates of U.S. medical schools choose more lucrative specialties instead.

When uninsurance rates are high, it's harder for even insured adults to get the health care they need.

The Uninsured Are Harmed the Most

Of course, the uninsured bear the brunt of the negative impact of lack of insurance. From 2000 to 2004, an IOM committee issued a landmark series of six reports on the consequences of uninsurance. As you'd expect, these reports confirmed that uninsured people, children and adults alike, have worse health and die sooner than do those with insurance. The final 2004 report recommended that the president and Congress develop a strategy to achieve universal coverage by 2010. Yet uninsurance has only risen, with no end in sight. Almost unwittingly, we have apparently accepted living with continuously rising rates of uninsurance.

The conventional wisdom has held that the United States has failed to address our uninsured crisis because people with insurance and the industry serving them refuse to give up their benefits or privileged positions. Many saw insuring the uninsured as an unnecessary and undesirable redistribution of wealth. But the IOM's most recent report questions this view.

And just in time: Right now our elected members of Congress along with President Obama are engaged with major health care players, attempting to fashion a plan for health care reform. Ideally, it will curtail overtreatment while extending coverage to all Americans. The IOM report tells us that we need a solution to America's uninsured crisis.

Too many Americans, more than one in six under age 65, are without health insurance. Universal access to adequate health insurance is clearly in the self-interest of all Americans, including those who now enjoy health insurance coverage, people who earn enough to be taxed under the new bill, and the providers of health services. It's good for all of us.

Health Care Reform Expands Coverage in the Wrong Way, by Sacrificing Quality of Care

Kathryn Nix

Kathryn Nix is a research assistant in the Center for Health Policy Studies at the Heritage Foundation, a conservative think tank.

The administration's health policy agenda—embodied in Congress's two giant health care bills (H.R.3590 and H.R.4872)—is now law. The justification for the new law's burdensome taxes, unprecedented mandates, deficit spending, and stifling government regulation is that millions of Americans will now be insured. But the real impact Obamacare will have on the uninsured is not what many Americans might have expected.

The Wrong Way to Expand Coverage

The Congressional Budget Office (CBO) is reporting that the new health care law will decrease the number of uninsured in 2019 by 32 million. However, this does not mean that universal coverage will be achieved—23 million Americans will remain without coverage, including illegal immigrants.

Of those Americans that do become insured, 16 million will be added to Medicaid, and 24 million will obtain coverage in the newly created exchanges. Moreover, an estimated 3 million Americans will lose their current employer-based insurance, and another 5 million will lose their current non-group or other form of coverage.

Obamacare expands coverage by increasing the size of government. Rather than making health insurance markets

Kathryn Nix, "Obamacare: Impact on the Uninsured," Heritage Foundation, April 20, 2010. Reprinted by permission.

more responsive to Americans' personal wants and needs, law-makers enacted a top-down approach that will impose their will on the rest of the country. This "reform" will result in less choice and competition for health care consumers and, although more Americans will be "covered," the quality of this coverage will decrease. Moreover, certain provisions of the new law will make obtaining health insurance *less* desirable by increasing costs, causing even more Americans to drop or lose coverage.

This "reform" will result in less choice and competition for health care consumers.

Millions of Americans Dumped into Medicaid

In order to cover low-income uninsured citizens, Obamacare expands eligibility for Medicaid to include all Americans that fall under 133 percent of the federal poverty level. However, Medicaid is a low-performing, low-quality federal program that fails to meet the needs of its beneficiaries. For example, Medicaid's failure to cover the cost to providers of seeing Medicaid patients has greatly reduced the number of doctors who will see Medicaid patients.

As a result, Medicaid beneficiaries have become even more reliant on emergency care than the uninsured. According to the Centers for Disease Control [and Prevention's] National Center for Health Statistics, Medicaid patients comprised 25.5 percent of all emergency room visits in 2006, while the uninsured made up only 17.4 percent. What is more, the emergency room visit rate among Medicaid patients was higher than that of the uninsured: Medicaid's emergency room visit rate was 82 per 100 Medicaid patients, while that of the uninsured was 48 per 100 uninsured patients.

Increasing the number of Americans reliant on Medicaid will further compound its current shortfalls. States are currently facing serious budget cuts due to decreasing revenues, a trend that is expected to continue in the years to come. Though under the new law, the federal government will cover the cost of expanding *benefits* in the initial years, states will have to pay the additional administrative costs of the expansion. And after 2017, the states will begin to pay a portion of the benefits expansion as well.

This increasing financial burden will force state legislators to make budget cuts, either to other state programs or to Medicaid itself, which would mean reduced benefits or even further reduced physician reimbursement rates. Both of these outcomes would be disastrous for Medicaid beneficiaries' access to quality care. Under the new law, the federal government will pay to increase primary care physician reimbursement rates to equal those paid by Medicare—but only for two years, leaving Medicaid in the same lurch it started in.

Finally, examples of state Medicaid expansions, such as the expansion of TennCare in Tennessee, have shown that adding the uninsured to Medicaid does not increase positive health outcomes. For instance, Heritage [Foundation's Center for] Health Policy [Studies] fellow Brian Blase found that following TennCare expansion, health outcomes in Tennessee actually deteriorated and Tennessee's mortality rate declined at a much slower rate than in surrounding states that did not expand their Medicaid programs.

Increasing Premiums Will Reduce the Number of Newly Insured

Strict new insurance regulations will cause the cost of coverage to skyrocket, encouraging the currently uninsured to remain uninsured. According to Heritage analysts Rea Hederman and Paul Winfree, attempting to micromanage the insurance industry by "trying to fix one flawed policy (the rating restrictions and guaranteed issue requirements) by adding another flawed policy (the mandate and costly subsidies) only makes the policy outcome even worse." In this case, bad policy will adversely affect the new law's ability to increase the number of insured.

A guaranteed-issue provision will allow Americans to wait until they are sick to seek out insurance, causing insurance premiums to soar. The individual mandate is intended to combat this by forcing Americans into the insurance market before they are sick. However, since the individual mandate penalty will be significantly less expensive than the cost of an insurance plan, this provision will not achieve universal coverage, and insurance risk pools will begin to consist more exclusively of only those who need insurance the most: the sick and the elderly. Younger, healthier Americans will likely choose to pay the penalty, purchasing insurance only if needed.

The effects this will have on premiums will be exacerbated by the inclusion of community rating, which forbids insurers to raise premiums for older patients more than three times the amount charged to younger patients. Young and healthy Americans will be the losers in this equation: The Associated Press predicts that health premiums for young adults will increase by 17 percent, causing fewer of them to purchase insurance.

Removing young and healthy patients from risk pools will in turn result in further premium increases, as only sick and elderly patients will be left, creating a "death spiral" as cause and effect intertwine to result in evermore increasing premiums, causing more Americans to drop coverage.

Finally, the new law requires that the Department of Health and Human Services mandate benefits and services that must be covered by all health plans. Increasing the value of all health plans will, of course, increase their cost, further aggravating the aforementioned problems.

Some Will Lose Current Coverage

The ranks of the currently uninsured will not simply be reduced by the new law. Rather, as millions of Americans find themselves newly covered, a substantial number will also find that they will lose the coverage they currently carry as a result of the health care overhaul. According to the CBO, 8–9 million Americans that currently receive employer-sponsored coverage will lose it. Of these, 1–2 million would go from receiving coverage from an employer to obtaining coverage through the exchanges.

> *More than half of the newly insured will find themselves subjected to the low-quality coverage offered by Medicaid.*

The source of the loss of employer-sponsored insurance is that, under the new law, businesses will pay a penalty of $2,000 for failing to offer insurance to their employees. However, as noted by Heritage analysts John Ligon and Robert Book, even if employers do offer insurance, if low-income employees are eligible to purchase insurance in the exchanges instead and opt to do so, the employer will pay a $3,000 fine. For employers who hire a high proportion of low-income workers, this creates a strong incentive to drop coverage altogether, much to the detriment of other employees who will not receive subsidies to purchase insurance in the exchanges.

Though the net effect of the new health care law will be to increase the number of insured, several million Americans will also lose their coverage as a direct effect of the federal overhaul. Many Americans who would not currently be able to call themselves uninsured may be surprised when they are able to do so in the years to come as a result of the president's health care agenda.

Not What Was Promised

President Obama and congressional leadership promised the American people health care reform that would increase access to health care while simultaneously creating greater choice and competition and curbing increasing health expenditures. Instead, lawmakers passed into law a top-down, heavy-handed government approach that will increase coverage at the expense of the other two objectives, instead limiting choice and increasing health spending.

Moreover, more than half of the newly insured will find themselves subjected to the low-quality coverage offered by Medicaid, and several provisions in the bill will either discourage the uninsured from seeking coverage or cause the insured to lose the coverage they currently have.

The PPACA Will Not Remedy Access and Quality Problems in Cancer Care

John Geyman

John Geyman is professor emeritus of family medicine at the University of Washington School of Medicine in Seattle, an author, and a frequent blogger at the website of Physicians for a National Health Program.

We ask the obvious question whether, and to what extent, the new health care law, the Patient Protection and Affordable Care Act of 2010 (PPACA), may help to alleviate . . . problems [of access and quality in cancer care].

On the potentially positive side of the ledger, PPACA will extend insurance coverage by 32 million people by 2019 (including 16 million on Medicaid); will provide subsidies starting in 2014 to help many lower-income people afford coverage; will eliminate cost sharing for many preventive services; will provide new funding to increase the capacity of community health centers; will put in place some limited reforms of the insurance industry, such as prohibiting exclusions based on preexisting conditions and banning annual and lifetime limits; and will establish a new nonprofit Patient-Centered Outcomes Research Institute charged with assessing the relative outcomes, effectiveness and appropriateness of different treatments.

Continuing Problems

All that might at first appear to remedy many of the system problems facing cancer patients, but this is unfortunately not the case, for these kinds of reasons.

John Geyman, "Will Health Care Reform 2010 Improve Access and Quality of Cancer Care?" Physicians for a National Health Program, August 8, 2010. Reprinted by permission.

1. At least 23 million people will still be uninsured in 2019, while tens of millions more will be underinsured. Exchanges don't become available to help the uninsured gain coverage for four more years, and even then that coverage may well be unaffordable for many. The individual mandate, as the primary lever to expand coverage in 2014, faces an uncertain future over constitutional challenges; 71 percent of Missouri voters have already opposed that mandate in a referendum. Medicaid expansion is delayed until 2014, and then will still be underfunded with many restrictions to care. As one example of recent cutbacks, the University Medical Center, as the only public oncology facility in Nevada, was shut down in 2009 leaving some 2,000 uninsured and underinsured cancer patients stranded. As the economic downturn continues and the states make further draconian cuts, we can only expect Medicaid coverage to become even less adequate.

2. The rapidly rising costs of cancer care keep going up unabated. Under PPACA, the market still rules on prices. The costs of cancer care increase by about 20 percent a year. Chemotherapy drugs lead the charge, and drug makers can set their prices with little restraint. As just one example, Ovation Pharmaceuticals raised the prices of four of its drugs by up to 3,436 percent (not a typo!) in 2006, including Cosmegen, its drug for Wilms' tumor, a cancer of the kidney in children. By 2007, three approved targeted drugs for cancer were costing about $100,000 a year. Other cancer treatments are also right up there. A course of proton beam therapy for prostate cancer (already overutilized beyond indications) costs about $50,000.

3. Health insurance and cancer care have become increasingly unaffordable for many patients and families. According to the Kaiser Family Foundation, the average premium for a family of four was $13,375 in 2009. Translating that to affordability terms, the Commonwealth Fund has developed criteria marking when payments become unaffordable, as measured against other essential costs of living—above 10 percent is

considered a financial hardship. That means that an annual household income of $130,000 a year would be required to cover health insurance without financial hardship, quite aside from the costs of health care ... if family members get sick! And the cost of health insurance is going up by 10 to 13 percent in 2010, depending on the type of plan. The PPACA will not help this problem. The Congressional Budget Office has projected that annual family insurance premiums in 2016 will cost more than $20,000, not including deductibles and other out-of-pocket costs, despite implementation of the new health care "reform" law. The actual costs of health care are an even bigger burden for patients and families than insurance, especially for cancer care. Even for those with insurance, out-of-pocket expenditures keep going up as more cost sharing is added through deductibles, co-payments and coinsurance. As the costs of chemotherapy drugs continue skyward, insurers typically require enrollees to pay coinsurance of 20 to 33 percent toward the cost of these drugs. If uninsured, the costs are even higher since hospitals typically charge them rates that are almost 2.5 those charged to insurers. Thomson Reuters reported in 2008 that one in four patients with advanced cancer with annual incomes less than $40,000 were refusing recommended treatment because of cost. And the recession of the last two years now finds an increasing number of patients reducing or stopping their life-extending chemotherapy drugs in hopes of their precious supplies lasting longer, but instead resulting in rapid regrowth of their cancers.

The rapidly rising costs of cancer care keep going up unabated.

---

4. The PPACA will end up reducing choice of coverage for many Americans. The exchanges will not be open for business until 2014, and then only for the uninsured and some small businesses. Affordability of adequate coverage through ex-

changes remains open to question. And for those already insured, the trend is toward more restricted choice. The country's biggest health insurers are now testing plans with tightly controlled networks of providers that will often force the insured to change physicians or pay much higher costs for the privilege of keeping their own doctors.

The main cost and affordability barriers will continue with little restraint so that many cancer patients will underuse essential care.

---

5. Insurance "reforms" won't prevent insurers from gaming the new system, maximizing their own profits as their under-insurance products become ever less adequate. Insurers still have many ways to get around some of the regulations put in place by the PPACA. For starters, existing insurance plans were grandfathered in without having to implement such requirements as stopping the use of preexisting conditions to deny coverage. Annual and lifetime caps won't be implemented until 2014; even then, existing plans are permanently exempted from both requirements. As the rules get written by the Department of Health and Human Services (HHS), insurers are lobbying hard for regulations least restrictive to their business practices, such as counting many administrative costs as direct patient care (e.g., calculations of medical loss ratios [MLRs], credentialing of physicians, quality assurance initiatives). They have wide latitude to set their premium rates despite the concerns of regulators. Plans can still deny coverage or even cancel policies. They have already forced the government to back-pedal on the requirement that they offer coverage to children up to 26 years of age on their parents' policies—insurers are now permitted to set limited sign-up periods for such coverage, such as just one month a year. In Florida, Blue Cross and Blue Shield, Aetna and Golden Rule (a subsidiary of

UnitedHealth) have notified the insurance commissioner that they will stop issuing individual policies for children.

One of the most critical rule-setting matters before HHS is the definition of minimal benefits, still pending. Many insurers now have fine-print restrictions in their policies that cancer patients find too late, such as steep surcharges for top-tier hospitals and higher coinsurance for Tier 4 chemotherapy drugs and radiation therapy. More than one-half of enrollees in private Medicare plans have no annual limits on their out-of-pocket costs, and many of these plans exclude coverage for chemotherapy.

6. The quality of cancer care will still suffer on two counts—the underuse of necessary care and the overuse of some services of marginal value that at times are even harmful. Although the PPACA may alleviate some of the access barriers for some cancer patients at least four years down the road, the main cost and affordability barriers will continue with little restraint so that many cancer patients will underuse essential care. Since most reimbursement policies are not significantly altered and perverse incentives for physicians and hospitals to provide more services will continue, overutilization of services of marginal value will remain a system problem. One common example makes the point. Radical prostatectomy is still performed in 60 percent of American men less than 75 years of age, often resulting in bowel, urinary or sexual dysfunction; many of these men did not need surgery in the first place. The new Patient-Centered Outcomes Research Institute will not be operational until near the end of this decade, and then will not be empowered to set coverage and reimbursement policies based on clinical efficacy and cost effectiveness.

So, back to our original question, in view of the above, we have to conclude that the new health care law, the PPACA, may make some marginal gains in a few areas, but will not remedy access and quality problems in cancer care, and will leave many patients and families in even more desperate straits than they are now. In essence—too little and too late.

The History of Health Coverage Expansion Shows That It Leads to Runaway Costs

Peter Suderman

Peter Suderman is associate editor of Reason *magazine.*

The [Patient Protection and] Affordable Care Act—otherwise known as Obamacare—isn't the first attempt to expand health insurance coverage in America. Before Washington passed its law, a number of states took smaller-scale cracks at the job—each of which proved far more expensive than planned. As the nation dives further into debt, the destabilizing fiscal effects of those programs don't bode well for how Obamacare will shape the U.S. budget.

Tennessee's Spectacular Failure

As spectacular failures go, it's hard to do worse than Tennessee. This early state attempt to dramatically increase health coverage, dubbed TennCare, started off promisingly. In 1994, the first year of its operation, the system added half a million new individuals to its rolls. Premiums were cheap—just $2.74 per month for people right above the poverty line—and liberal policy wonks loved it. The Urban Institute, for example, gave it good marks for "improving coverage of the uninsurable or high-risk individuals with very limited access to private coverage." At its peak, the program covered 1.4 million individuals—nearly a quarter of the state's population and more than any other state's Medicaid program—leaving just 6 percent of the state's population uninsured.

Peter Suderman, "Health Care's History of Fiscal Folly: Expanding Health Coverage Busted State Budgets. Will It Bust the Federal Budget Too?" *Reason*, April 7, 2010. Reprinted by permission of Reason magazine and Reason.com

But those benefits came at a high price. By 2001, the system's costs were growing faster than the state budget. The drive to increase coverage had not been matched by the drive to control costs. Vivian Riefberg, a partner at consulting firm McKinsey & Company, described it as having "almost across the board, no limits on scope and duration of coverage." Spending on drug coverage, in particular, had gone out of control: The state topped the nation in prescription drug use, and the program put no cap on how many prescription drugs a patient could receive. The result was that, by 2004, TennCare's drug benefits cost the state more than its entire higher education program. Meanwhile, in 1998, the program was opened to individuals at twice the poverty level, even if they had access to employer-provided insurance.

The Massachusetts . . . health care program has success- fully expanded coverage . . . but the price tag may be more than the state can bear.

In other words, the program's costs were uncontrolled and unsustainable. By 2004, the budget had jumped from $2.6 billion to $6.9 billion, and it accounted for a quarter of the state's appropriations. A McKinsey report projected that the program's costs could hit $12.8 billion by 2008, consuming 36 percent of state appropriations and 91 percent of new state tax revenues. On the question of the system's fiscal sustainability, the report concluded that, even if a number of planned reforms were implemented, the program would simply "not be financially viable."

Democratic Gov. Phil Bredesen declared the report "sobering," and, rather than allow the state to face bankruptcy, quickly scaled the state back to a traditional Medicaid model, dropping about 200,000 from the program in a period of about four months. Though the state still calls its Medicaid program TennCare, Bredesen's decision to scale back effectively shut the program down. In 2007, he told the journal *Health Affairs*, "The idea of TennCare, as it was implemented, failed."

Another Failure in Maine

Maine took a different route to expanding coverage, but it also resulted in failure. In 2003, the state started Dirigo Care, which, it was promised, would cover each and every one of the state's 128,000 uninsured by 2009. The program was given a one-time $53 million grant to get things started, but was intended to be eventually self-sustaining. It wasn't. Indeed, the program managed the neat trick of drastically overshooting cost projections while drastically undershooting coverage estimates.

If Obamacare's actual fiscal effects look anything like previous efforts to expand health coverage, the federal budget is in for a world of hurt.

In 2009, the year in which the program was to have successfully covered all of the uninsured, the uninsured rate still hovered around 10 percent—effectively unchanged from when the program began. Taxpayers and insurers, however, had picked up an additional $155 million in unexpected costs—all while the state was wading deeper into massive budget shortfalls and increased debt. The program has not been shut down, but because expected cost savings did not materialize, it's been all but abandoned. As of September 2009, only 9,600 individuals remained covered through the plan.

The Expensive Massachusetts Plan

And then there is the Massachusetts plan, the model for Obamacare. The state's health care program has successfully expanded coverage to about 97 percent of the state's population, but the price tag may be more than the state can bear.

When the program was signed into law, estimates indicated that the cost of its health insurance subsidies would be about $725 million per year. But by 2008, those projections had been revised. New estimates indicated that the plan was to cost $869 million in 2009 and $880 million in 2010, an upward increase of nearly 20 percent. More recently, the governor's office announced a $294 million shortfall on health care funds, and state health insurance commissioners have warned that, on its current course, the program may be headed for bankruptcy. According to an analysis by the RAND Corporation, "in the absence of policy change, health care spending in Massachusetts is projected to nearly double to $123 billion in 2020, increasing 8 percent faster than the state's gross domestic product (GDP)." The state's treasurer, a former Democrat who recently split with his party, says that the program has survived only because of federal assistance.

Defenders of the program argue that it's not really a budget buster because the state's budget was already in trouble. But for those worried about Obamacare's potential effects on the federal budget, that's hardly comforting. The Congressional Budget Office (CBO) has warned that, without significant change, the U.S. fiscal situation is "unsustainable," with publicly held debt likely to reach a potentially destabilizing 90 percent of GDP by 2020. Democrats managed to get the CBO to score Obamacare as a net reduction in the deficit, but those projections are tremendously uncertain at best. As [former chairman of the Federal Reserve] Alan Greenspan warned last weekend [August 2008], if the CBO's estimates are wrong, the consequences could be "severe."

The history of health coverage expansion should make us worry. If Obamacare's actual fiscal effects look anything like previous efforts to expand health coverage, the federal budget is in for a world of hurt.

Health Care Reform Is a Disaster for All Americans

Peter Ferrara

Peter Ferrara is director of entitlement and budget policy at the Institute for Policy Innovation; a policy advisor to the Heartland Institute; a senior fellow at the Social Security Institute; and general counsel of the American Civil Rights Union. He served in the White House Office of Policy Development under President Reagan and as associate deputy attorney general of the United States under the first President Bush.

[The Heartland Institute, a conservative policy research group, has released] my extensive study of the Obamacare legislation, *The Obamacare Disaster: An Appraisal of the Patient Protection and Affordable Care Act*, available . . . at the Heartland Institute website. Following [House Speaker] Nancy Pelosi's dictum that we will have to pass it first to know what's in it, I personally slogged through the thousands of pages of this legislative atrocity for the study, as well as thousands of pages of supplemental materials such as government, think tank and media reports.

The bottom line is that you will lose your health care under this legislation, if not your job, your country as they bankrupt America, and maybe ultimately your life or the life of a loved one. All that to make dreamy, emotionalized liberals happy, even though many of them are not happy because the socialism in the bill is not overt enough. Moreover, the promises made to the American people to pass the bill are shown in the study to be thoroughly false. This pattern of calculated deception, however, did not fool the American people, only members of Congress, many of whom will now pay with *their* jobs as a result.

Peter Ferrara, "The Right Prescription: The Obamacare Disaster," *American Spectator*, August 18, 2010. Reprinted by permission.

But the study is not all gloom and doom. It thoroughly explains the patient power reforms that should replace it when it is repealed, drawing on the broad scholarship of the patient power movement and its intellectual leaders, such as John Goodman, Grace-Marie Turner, Sally Pipes, Merrill Matthews, and Greg Scandlen, among others. It consequently serves as a guidebook for the grassroots Tea Party activists who will lead the long-term crusade for health care liberation.

You will lose your health care under this legislation.

The Government Takeover of Health Care

Contrary to President Obama's rhetoric, the Obamacare legislation involves precisely the thorough government takeover of health care. It creates 159 new bureaucracies, agencies, boards, commissions, and programs to rule over health care in America. Government authorities are empowered to tell doctors and hospitals what is quality health care and what is not, what are best practices in medicine, how their medical practices should be structured, and what they will be paid and when. Government authorities will mandate exactly what health insurance with what benefits workers and employers must buy, and the act imposes tax penalties on them if they do not comply. Government authorities will dictate to insurance companies exactly what health insurance they must sell, to whom they must sell it, and what they can charge. Obamacare even redistributes premium income among insurers under a new "risk adjustment" mechanism.

But this is just the beginning. As in everything President Obama is doing, it lays the groundwork for much more thorough government control and compulsion over time, primarily through bureaucratic land mines involving grants of regulatory authority that will explode when the bureaucracy thinks it can get away with it politically. Among the biggest targets here will be doctors and hospitals, which over time will become complete vassals of the regulatory, bureaucratic state Obamacare establishes.

Higher Health Care Costs

President Obama promised while campaigning for his health reform legislation that it would reduce the "growth of health care costs for our families, our businesses, and our government," in particular by reducing the cost of health insurance by $2,500 per family. But the Obamacare legislation will have just the opposite effect, sharply increasing health costs for families, businesses, and government.

Obamacare will sharply increase insurance costs [beginning] ... with the mandates forcing everyone into comprehensive insurance coverage.

Higher costs for government start with the expansion of the Medicaid entitlement, which was already slated to cost $5 trillion over the next 10 years. The Centers for Medicare and Medicaid Services estimates that Obamacare will increase Medicaid enrollment by 24 million new beneficiaries by 2015, adding an additional $410 billion in further federal costs for the program over the next decade alone.

Obamacare increases costs for the federal government further by adopting a massive new health insurance entitlement program for families earning up to four times the poverty level. In 2014, this new program will be providing $3,000 in taxpayer funds to families making $95,000. By 2018, almost $5,000 will be going to families making $102,000. CBO [Congressional Budget Office] estimates that these subsidies will cost taxpayers an additional $457 billion over the first six years alone, through 2019. The chief actuary of Medicare estimates the total cost of this new entitlement will reach over

$500 billion over the first six years. This is only the beginning, as this program will ultimately cost far more than now projected.

This is a massive increase in welfare extended to middle- and upper-income families, irresponsibly added on top of the runaway, financially intractable entitlement promises we have already made. But Obamacare then adds a third new entitlement program, for long-term nursing home care.

For the rest of us, Obamacare will sharply increase insurance costs. That starts with the mandates forcing everyone into comprehensive insurance coverage specified by the government, which will maximize the incentives for overconsumption of health care, to be paid for through the insurance. Then there are all of President Obama's free new benefits now mandated, such as coverage for alcohol and drug abuse rehab, mental health services, preventive care, maternity benefits for single males and postmenopausal adults, and the elimination of all lifetime limits and caps. Free mandatory benefits raise health insurance costs.

Several provisions of Obamacare give insurers, doctors, and hospitals incentives to deny and ration health care to patients.

Additional regulatory burdens will further increase costs. The guaranteed issue requirements force insurers to issue new policies to anyone who applies regardless of how sick they are, and the community rating requirements prohibit charging them more because of their illnesses. These requirements, which are just like forcing fire insurers to issue new policies to applicants whose houses are already on fire when they call, at regular rates, raise the costs of health insurance sharply for everyone else.

Two new taxes on health insurance, the Cadillac tax for supposedly high-value insurance that will apply to more and more plans every year, and another tax on all health insurance from the start, will add nearly $100 billion to health insurance costs over the next 10 years alone. Then there will be sharply increased cost shifting to private health insurance due to the massive expansion of Medicaid to 24 million more people, and the more than massive Medicare cuts discussed below, as doctors and hospitals try to recoup their enormous losses by charging more to privately insured patients.

Counting just some of these cost increases, one study concludes that under Obamacare a typical family health insurance policy costing $12,300 today will cost $17,200 by 2013, $21,300 by 2016, and $25,900 by 2019. Another study concludes that insurance costs for young (up to 40) and healthy workers will double and triple in many cases.

These cost increases have already begun. But expect the liberal/left to insist that the soaring insurance costs caused by Obamacare prove that the public option, or even more overt socialized medicine, was needed after all. They will seek to prohibit the necessary premium increases, as in Massachusetts, and will be glad if that forces private insurers out of business.

Death Panels

While the liberal/left hides behind literal clowns mocking Sarah Palin for raising the issue of death panels under Obamacare, the legislation as passed documents the essential reality of the charge.

The recently released annual report of the Medicare Board of Trustees reveals that the Medicare payment rates for the doctors and hospitals serving seniors will be cut by 30% over the next 3 years. By 2019, those Medicare payment rates will be lower than under Medicaid. The chief actuary for Medicare reports that ultimately under Obamacare Medicare payment rates will be only one-third of what will be paid by private insurance and only half of what is paid by Medicaid, where the poor often can't find access to essential care.

Still further Medicare cuts adopted in the Obamacare legislation add up altogether to $818 billion over the first 10 years of full implementation, 2014–2023, and $3.223 trillion over the first 20 years, 2014–2033, *for Medicare Part A alone!* Adding in the cuts for Medicare Part B brings the total to $1.048 trillion over the first 10 full years, and $4.95 trillion over the first 20 full years. Eventually, as documented in the government's own reports, Medicare Part A is cut by 60% per year, Part B by 43%!

These draconian cuts for doctors and hospitals providing the health care to seniors under Medicare were the basis for the CBO score repeatedly cited by President Obama that Obamacare would actually reduce the deficit while expanding or adopting three entitlement programs. This doesn't even include the further cuts to Medicare Advantage, the private alternative to Medicare which nearly 25% of seniors have chosen for their Medicare coverage because it gives them a better deal, and the further automatic Medicare cuts to be adopted by the unelected, appointed, bureaucrats at the Medicare Independent Payment Advisory Board under Obamacare.

Such draconian Medicare cuts would create havoc and chaos in health care for seniors. Doctors, hospitals, surgeons and specialists providing critical care to the elderly such as surgery for hip and knee replacements, sophisticated diagnostics through MRIs and CT scans, and even treatment for cancer and heart disease will shut down and disappear in much of the country, and others will stop serving Medicare patients. If the government is not going to pay, then seniors are not going to get the health services, treatment and care they expect. Indeed, the Medicare chief actuary reports that even before these cuts already two-thirds of hospitals were losing money on Medicare patients. Health providers will either have to withdraw from serving Medicare patients, or eventually go into bankruptcy.

Apparently, President Obama's concept of spreading the wealth includes sacking the Medicare system on which America's seniors have come to rely for highly beneficial medical care, in favor of others who the Obama/Pelosi/[Senate Majority Leader Harry] Reid progressive vision deems more worthy.

As the government clamps down on private insurers as well as on payments from Medicare and Medicaid, the incentives for essential investment to maintain current facilities, expand and open new ones, and invest in and build out new innovations and breakthroughs, will be eviscerated. Investment in human capital as well as physical capital in health care will plummet, as doctors and other professionals increasingly flee health care. This effective decline in the supply of health care in the face of increasing demand will mean even higher prices and costs.

The study further explains how several provisions of Obamacare give insurers, doctors, and hospitals incentives to deny and ration health care to patients. A central component of the traditional high standard of living in America has been the best, most advanced, cutting-edge health care in the world. No more. Obamacare is part of the declining standard of living for America.

America's Coming Bankruptcy

When he was campaigning for Obamacare, President Obama insisted on national television that the mandate to buy insurance was not a tax. Now that it has passed, his lawyers are in court arguing that it is constitutional because it is a tax.

The mandate to buy insurance is economically, though not legally, indistinguishable from a tax. Even with the budget-crushing new entitlement subsidies in the act, the insurance will be quite expensive, ranging up to 2 percent of income for people at 133 percent of poverty to 9.8 percent of income for people at 400 percent of poverty. That is like a new payroll tax, breaking two Obama pledges, since it applies just as well to those making less than $250,000 a year.

The study recounts at least 13 tax increases in Obamacare, adding up to at least $500 billion over the first 10 years, not counting the mandates. But that won't begin to cover all of the spending involved in Obamacare, adding up to more than $2.4 trillion over the first 10 years of full implementation, from 2014 to 2024, and $5.3 trillion over the first 15 full years.

That will further explode the deficit and national debt by at least $2 to $3 trillion over the next 20 years. A major fallacy of the CBO score of Obamacare is that it assumes that only 19 million workers will qualify for the new Obamacare health insurance subsidies described above. In fact, as former CBO Chief Douglas Holtz-Eakin explains . . . at least 43 million are likely to qualify. It could be 2 to 3 times as many, exploding original cost projections beyond imagination. The study explains other factors that will cause higher Obamacare spending and deficits. This would only follow the Medicare precedent, which was originally projected in 1965 to cost $12 trillion by 1990. But when 1990 came, it cost $109.7 billion, 9 times greater.

Patient Power v. Government Power

America does need to ensure that it maintains a health care safety net assuring that no one suffers due to lack of essential health care. But that can be accomplished without any of the big-government components of Obamacare. Indeed, done right, it can be accomplished while expanding the power and control of workers and patients over their own health care and actually reducing rather than enlarging government's role in health care.

That would begin by repealing all 159 new bureaucracies, agencies, boards, commissions and programs created by Obamacare and the rest of the legislative atrocity, reducing taxes and spending by the amounts described above and the federal deficits and debt by at least $2 to $3 trillion over the next 20 years.

The next step would be to block grant Medicaid back to the states following the model of the hugely successful 1996 reforms of the old AFDC [Aid to Families with Dependent Children] program. That would greatly benefit the poor, freeing them from the Medicaid ghetto to enjoy the same health insurance as the middle class. That would include the choice of health savings accounts (HSAs), maximizing patient power and control, and market incentives to control costs. Medicare should be reformed to empower all seniors with a Medicare Advantage choice, including the highly beneficial HSAs.

A true health care safety net ensuring essential health care for all can be achieved with state high-risk pools and consumer choice tax credits, ensuring affordability and access to health insurance for everyone. . . .

Because of all of the problems created by Obamacare, the misshapen legislation is just the beginning, not the end, of the battle to reform health care policy in America. Obamacare is so fundamentally wrongheaded that it takes us in the opposite direction of the essential reforms that are needed. Perhaps such a disastrously wrong step was necessary to draw the public's attention to the true patient power reforms that would liberate health care in America.

Organizations to Contact

The editors have compiled the following list of organizations concerned with the issues debated in this book. The descriptions are derived from materials provided by the organizations. All have publications or information available for interested readers. The list was compiled on the date of publication of the present volume; the information provided here may change. Be aware that many organizations take several weeks or longer to respond to inquiries, so allow as much time as possible.

American Medical Association (AMA)
515 N. State Street, Chicago, IL   60654
(800) 621-8335
website: www.ama-assn.org

The American Medical Association (AMA) is the largest medical association of physicians in the nation. It represents physicians from every state and specialty and works to promote the art and science of medicine and the betterment of public health. The AMA supports meaningful health system reform, and its website contains information, analysis, and articles for physicians and patients about the AMA's position on reform and the impact of the 2010 health care reform law.

Campaign for an American Solution
(800) 289-1136
e-mail: info@americanhealthsolution.org
website: www.americanhealthsolution.org

The Campaign for an American Solution is a nonpartisan, educational initiative of America's Health Insurance Plans (AHIP), the national trade association for the health insurance industry. The mission of the initiative is to build support for health care reforms favored by insurance companies. The website is a source of information about the industry's views on health care reform, and it contains documents such as position statements, congressional testimony, and links to studies on health care costs.

Cato Institute

1000 Massachusetts Avenue NW
Washington, DC   20001-5403
(202) 842-0200 • fax: (202) 842-3490
website: www.cato.org

The Cato Institute is a libertarian public policy research foundation headquartered in Washington, D.C. Cato's mission is to promote public policies based on the principles of limited government, free markets, individual liberty, and peace. The group publishes a variety of publications including books, monographs, briefing papers, and shorter studies, in addition to the quarterly magazine *Regulation* and the bimonthly *Cato Policy Report* newsletter. A search of the Cato website reveals a list of publications relating to the uninsured and health care reform. Examples include "Bad Medicine: A Guide to the Real Costs and Consequences of the New Health Care Law" and "Bending the Productivity Curve: Why America Leads the World in Medical Innovation."

Center for American Progress (CAP)

1333 H Street NW, 10th Floor, Washington, DC   20005
(202) 682-1611 • fax: (202) 682-1867
website: www.americanprogress.org

The Center for American Progress (CAP) is a progressive think tank that works on issues such as energy, national security, economic growth and opportunity, immigration, education, and health care. CAP develops new policy ideas, critiques policies being considered by policy makers, and challenges the media to cover the issues that truly matter. The group produces numerous reports and policy papers addressing health care. Recent publications include "A Step-by-Step Look at How Health Reform Covers Everyone While Saving Us Money" and "Good Health, Good Jobs."

Center on Budget and Policy Priorities

820 First Street NE, Suite 510, Washington, DC 20002
(202) 408-1080 • fax: (202) 408-1056
e-mail: center@cbpp.org
website: www.cbpp.org

The Center on Budget and Policy Priorities is a policy research organization that works at federal and state levels on fiscal policy and public programs that affect low- and moderate-income families and individuals. The center conducts research and analysis to help shape public debates over proposed budget and tax policies and to help ensure that policy makers consider the needs of low-income families and individuals in these debates. One of the group's main areas of research is health care, and this section of its website contains numerous articles, analyses, and other publications about health care reform, the impact of the 2010 health care law, and other health issues.

Commonwealth Fund

One East Seventy-fifth Street, New York, NY 10021
(212) 606-3800 • fax: (212) 606-3500
website: www.commonwealthfund.org

The Commonwealth Fund is a private foundation that promotes health care reform to achieve better access, improved quality, and greater efficiency, particularly for low-income people, the uninsured, minority Americans, young children, and elderly adults. The fund carries out this mandate by supporting independent research on health care issues and making grants to improve health care practice and policy. The fund produces more than one hundred free publications a year, including several newsletters and an online annual report. Recent publications include "Achieving the Vision: Payment Reform" and "Why the Nation Needs a Policy Push on Patient-Centered Health Care."

Institute of Medicine (IOM)

500 Fifth Street NW, Washington, DC   20001
(202) 334-2352
e-mail: iomwww@nas.edu
website: www.iom.edu

The Institute of Medicine (IOM) is an independent, nonprofit organization that works outside of government to provide unbiased and authoritative advice to decision makers and the public. Established in 1970, the IOM is the health arm of the National Academy of Sciences, which was chartered under President Abraham Lincoln in 1863 to provide advice to the nation about various sciences. The IOM studies health issues, often as a mandate from Congress or as requested by federal agencies and independent organizations, and prepares reports of its findings (available on its website). The IOM also convenes a series of forums, roundtables, and standing committees to facilitate discussion, discovery, and critical cross-disciplinary thinking.

Kaiser Family Foundation—Health Care Reform

2400 Sand Hill Road, Menlo Park, CA   94025
(650) 854-9400 • fax: (650) 854-4800
website: http://healthreform.kff.org

The Kaiser Family Foundation is a nonprofit, private operating foundation focusing on the major health care issues facing the United States as well as the US role in global health policy. Unlike grant-making foundations, Kaiser develops and runs its own research and communications programs, sometimes in partnership with other nonprofit research organizations or major media companies. The foundation serves as a nonpartisan source of facts, information, and analysis about health care reform for policy makers, the media, the health care community, and the public. Its website contains a wide range of information including analyses of the new health care law, issue briefs about health care matters, results of public opinion polls, and congressional testimony.

Physicians for a National Health Program (PNHP)
29 E Madison, Suite 602, Chicago, IL   60602
(312) 782-6006 • fax: (312) 782-6007
e-mail: info@pnhp.org
website: www.pnhp.org

Physicians for a National Health Program (PNHP) is a single issue organization that advocates for a universal, comprehensive single-payer national health program. With more than seventeen thousand members and chapters across the United States, the group seeks to educate physicians and other health professionals about the benefits of a single-payer system—including fewer administrative costs and affordable health insurance for the 46 million Americans who have none. The PNHP website includes articles about health reform, and the group also publishes a newsletter (for members only), a blog, and press releases.

Bibliography

Books

Henry J. Aaron and William B. Schwartz, with Melissa Cox
Can We Say No?: The Challenge of Rationing Health Care. Washington, DC: Brookings Institution Press, 2005.

Donald L. Barlett and James B. Steele
Critical Condition: How Health Care in America Became Big Business—and Bad Medicine. New York: Broadway Books, 2005.

David Blumenthal and James Morone
The Heart of Power: Health and Politics in the Oval Office. Berkeley, CA: University of California Press, 2009.

David S. Broder and Haynes Johnson
The System: The American Way of Politics at the Breaking Point. New York: Back Bay Books, 1996.

Michael F. Cannon
Healthy Competition: What's Holding Back Health Care and How to Free It. 2nd ed. Washington, DC: Cato Institute, 2007.

Jonathan Cohn
Sick: The Untold Story of America's Health Care Crisis—and the People Who Pay the Price. New York: HarperCollins, 2007.

Stephen M. Davidson
Still Broken: Understanding the U.S. Health Care System. Stanford, CA: Stanford University Press, 2010.

Howard Dean
with Igor Volsky
and Faiz Shakir

Howard Dean's Prescription for Real Healthcare Reform: How We Can Achieve Affordable Medical Care for Every American and Make Our Jobs Safer. White River Junction, VT: Chelsea Green Publishing, 2009.

David Gratzer

The Cure: How Capitalism Can Save American Health Care. New York: Encounter Books, 2006.

Regina E.
Herzlinger

Who Killed Health Care?: America's $2 Trillion Medical Problem and the Consumer-Driven Cure. New York: McGraw-Hill, 2007.

Steven Jonas,
Raymond
Goldsteen, and
Karen Goldsteen

An Introduction to the U.S. Health Care System. 6th ed. New York: Springer Publishing Company, 2007.

Jon Kallberg

How Socialized Health Care Will Radically Change America—Why Universal Health Care Will Create a Political Hegemony as in Sweden. Dallas, TX: Railhead Publishing, 2010.

Peter R.
Kongstvedt

Managed Care: What It Is and How It Works. 3rd ed. Sudbury, MA: Jones & Bartlett Publishers, 2009.

Robert H. LeBow

Health Care Meltdown: Confronting the Myths and Fixing Our Failing System. Chambersburg, PA: A.C. Hood, 2004.

T.R. Reid — *The Healing of America: A Global Quest for Better, Cheaper, and Fairer Health Care*. New York: Penguin Press, 2009.

Arnold S. Relman — *A Second Opinion: Rescuing America's Healthcare: A Plan for Universal Coverage Serving Patients over Profit*. New York: PublicAffairs, 2010.

Saul William Seidman — *Trillion Dollar Scam: Exploding Health Care Fraud*. Boca Raton, FL: Universal Publishers, 2008.

Leiyu Shi and Douglas A. Singh — *Essentials of the U.S. Health Care System*. Sudbury, MA: Jones & Bartlett Publishers, 2010.

Staff of the Washington Post — *Landmark: The Inside Story of America's New Health-Care Law and What It Means for Us All*. New York: Public Affairs, 2010.

Periodicals

Catherine Arnst — "Health Care: Not So Recession-Proof," *Bloomberg Businessweek*, March 25, 2008.

Atul Gawande — "The Cost Conundrum," *New Yorker*, June 1, 2009.

David Goldhill — "How American Health Care Killed My Father," *Atlantic*, September 2009.

Phillip Longman — "Best Care Everywhere," *Washington Monthly*, October 2007.

Theodore Marmor, Jonathan Oberlander, and Joseph White — "The Obama Administration's Options for Health Care Cost Control: Hope Versus Reality," *Annals of Internal Medicine*, April 7, 2009.

Megan McArdle — "The Future After Health Care," *Atlantic*, March 21 2010.

Kate Michelman — "A System from Hell," *Nation*, April 8, 2009.

Timothy Noah — "A Short History of Health Care," *Slate*, March 13, 2007.

Timothy Noah — "Health Reform: An Online Guide: Links to Everything You Need to Know About the Patient Protection and Affordable Care Act of 2010," *Slate*, May 13, 2010.

Martin Peretz — "Do You Want a Really Excellent Medical System? Live in Israel or at Least Learn About 'Health Care for All' in the Jewish State," *New Republic*, May 20, 2010.

Harold Pollack — "Will Lack of Insurance Kill You?" *New Republic*, February 18, 2010.

Steven Reinberg — "Recession Scrambling Health Spending in U.S.," *U.S. News & World Report*, February 24, 2009.

James Ridgeway — "Meet the Real Death Panels: Should Geezers Like Me Give Up Life-Prolonging Treatments to Cut Health Care Costs?" *Mother Jones*, July/August 2010.

Katharine Q.
Seelye
"A Constitutional Debate over a Health Care Mandate," *New York Times*, September 26, 2009.

Jacob Sullum
"Don't Buy It: The Crazy Constitutional Logic of the Individual Insurance Mandate," *Reason*, March 24, 2010.

June Thomas
"The American Way of Dentistry," *Slate*, September 28, 2009.

Karen Tumulty
"Making History: House Passes Health Care Reform," *Time*, March 23, 2010.

Brad Tuttle
"So Are Health Insurance Rates Bound to Skyrocket Now or What?" *Time*, March 24, 2010.

Glen Whitman
"Hazards of the Individual Health Care Mandate," *Cato Policy Report*, September/October 2007.

Index

A

Abdullah, Dr. Fizan, 26
"Accidents, Murders, Preemies, Fat, and US Life Expectancy" (Bailey), 77–78
Acquired immunodeficiency disease (AIDS), 74
Adults with continuous insurance, 60, 61–62
Adults without insurance
    decreased physical checkups, 60
    difficulties obtaining insurance, 56
    evidence of declining health, 55
    harmfulness of, 52
    low self-perceived wellness levels, 58–59
    risks of death, 56, 59
    sources of insurance for, 53–54
Aetna insurance company, 19, 74
AFDC (Aid to Families with Dependent Children) program, 163
Affordable Health Insurance program, 131
African Americans, uninsured data, 23
Alaska Natives, uninsured data, 23
Altman, Drew, 79–82
American Cancer Society (ACS)
    analysis of cancer cases, 65
    insurance -cancer-survival study, 67–68
    study of uninsured patients, 66

American Civil Rights Union, 155
American Journal of Medicine, 28
Anthem insurance company, 79–80
"Association of Insurance with Cancer Care Utilization and Outcomes" study, 6565
At-risk populations, 58, 595
Autism, 74

B

"Bad Medicine" (Cato Institute report), 101
Bailey, Ronald, 76–78
Bailey v. Drexel Furniture Co. (1920), 120
Bankruptcies. *See* Medical bankruptcies
Barnett, Randy, 118–122
Baylor Hospital (Texas), 18
Bernstein, Jill, 58–64
Blue Cross health insurance
    experience-rating model, 19
    origination of, 18
Brawley, Otis, 68
Bredesen, Phil, 152–153
Brookings Institute, 128
Bundorf, M. Kate, 43
Bush, George H.W., 155
Bush, George W., 96, 155

C

CA: A Cancer Journal For Clinicians, 65
"Cadillac" insurance plans, 84

California
Anthem premium increase, 79–80
immigrant hospital care, 93
Los Angeles uninsured rates, 56
Callahan, Daniel, 87
Cancer patients (with/without insurance), 60
ACS research analysis, 65
insurance status, diagnosis, survival, 67–68
limitations of PPACA, 145–150
national health survey/cancer prevention, 66–67
risks of death, 65–68
Cannon, Michael, 35
Cardiovascular disease, 55
Cato Institute, 35, 101
Census Bureau (US), uninsured data, 17, 22–23, 42
Center for American Progress, 35
Center for Health Policy Studies (Heritage Foundation), 141
Center for Studying Health System Change (HSC), 58
Centers for Disease Control and Prevention (CDC), 65, 140
Century Foundation research institution, 69
Chang, David C., 25, 26–27
Chemerinsky, Erwin, 107–110
Children without insurance
Johns Hopkins study, 26–27
lack of access to services, 60
likelihood of hospital death, 25–27
medical care deficiencies, 59
smoke screen effect, 42–43
vulnerability of, 40

Chollet, Deborah, 58–64
Chronic obstructive pulmonary disease (COPD), 55
Cohn, Jonathan, 83, 97–100
Collins, Sara R., 131–135
Commerce Clause (US Constitution), 117, 119–122
Commonwealth Fund research organization, 131
Communities
at-risk communities, 55–57
attractiveness based on insurance, 61
community-based services, 60
consequences of uninsured, 63
minority-based (US), 85
uninsurance rates, 52
Community rate premium system, 18–19, 44, 56
Congress (US)
citizen view of, 46
emergency treatment legislation, 99
exercise of tax and spend power, 109–110
Health Maintenance Organization Act, 20
Internal Revenue Code mandate, 121–122
PPACA/ individual responsibility justification, 119
PPACA/health reform authority, 118
Second Congress/Militia Act (of 1792), 114–117
1792 "individual mandate," 104–106
Congressional Budget Office (CBO)
decreased uninsured projections, 139

employer-sponsored insurance losses, 143

family insurance premium estimates, 147

PPACA health coverage estimates, 126, 139

premium coverage study, 81

score for Obamacare, 160, 162

study of uninsured people, 43

taxpayer subsidy estimates, 157

warnings about US fiscal system, 154

Constitution (US)

Commerce Clause, 117, 119–122

individual insurance mandate questions, 107–110

interstate commerce regulation, 107

invocation of power of, 109–110

Militia Act (of 1792), 114–116

offenses of individual mandate, 114

Tenth Amendment, 105

Consumer Operated and Oriented Plans (CO-OPs), 63

ConsumerAffairs.com, 28–30

Continuous coverage health insurance, 61–62

Costs of health insurance. *See* Health insurance premiums

Cuccinelli, Ken, 114

D

Death from lack of insurance

cancer deaths, 65–68

children in hospitals, 25–27

death with insurance vs., 35–41, 54

IOM data, 83–84

lack of risk from death, 39–41

premature deaths, 55, 58–59, 61–62, 69, 73, 103

smoking deaths vs., 86–87

specific disease risks, 71–72

University of Pennsylvania study, 76

Democratic Party

criticism of, 45

emergency treatment legislation, 99

in favor of health plan, 46

limited knowledge of uninsured, 36

universal coverage concerns, 46–47

Department of Health and Human Services (HHS), 142, 148

Department of Veterans Affairs, 92

Dirigo Care (Maine), 153

"Don't Ask, Don't Tell" (military homosexual policy), 113

Doty, Michelle M., 131–135

E

eHealthInsurance.com, 80

Electronic medical records, 129

Emergency Medical Treatment and Active Labor Act, 99

Employer-based health insurance, 23

consequences of loss, 35

health care crisis caused by, 20

male vs. female coverage, 33

Obama/PPACA and, 20, 125

out-of-pocket payments, 50–51, 79

US recession, 31

World War II onset, 19

See also Private insurance

Engelberg Center for Health Care Reform, 128

Evidence-based treatment improvements, 129–130

F

Family and Preventive Medicine Department (UC, San Diego), 39

Federal poverty level (FPL) Medicaid eligibility, 63

Federal Reserve (US), 154

Ferrara, Peter, 155–163

First Focus child/family advocacy group, 26

The Foundry blog (Heritage Foundation), 114

FOX News, interview with Romney, 100

G

Geyman, John, 145–150

Goodman, John, 156

Greenspan, Alan, 154

H

Hardship exemptions (from PPACA), 92

Harvard Medical School, 28

Health Affairs journal, 153

Health care system (US)
citizen ratings, 47
for-profit model, 19–20
global comparisons, 17–18
IOM recommendations, 57
political party opinions, 46
See also Employer-based health insurance; Patient Protection and Affordable Care Act; Private insurance

Health Connector program (Massachusetts), 94–95

Health insurance
"Cadillac" insurance plans, 84
children/adult well-being from, 52–57
continuous coverages, 61–62
downward coverage spiral, 53–54
drug coverage, 62
employer-based, 23
expansion and runaway costs, 151–154
family premiums, 22
global consequences of lack of, 61
health benefits relation to, 69–75, 83–86
importance of coverage, 54–55
influence on interstate commerce, 107–109
Kronick/RAND studies, 39–40, 70–71, 84–85
lives saved by, 86
mental health coverage, 62–63
onset during Great Depression, 18
potential loss from PPACA, 143
preventive service coverage, 62
relation to outcomes, 58–64
sociodemographic characteristics, 67
value of, 25–26
See also Employer-based health insurance; High deductible insurance; Medicaid program; Medicare program; Patient Protection and Affordable Care Act; Private insurance

Health insurance premiums
  Anthem California increase,
    79–80
  CBO family insurance esti-
    mates, 147
  community rate premium
    system, 18–19, 44, 56
  consequences to newly in-
    sured, 141–142
  costs vs. lack of coverage
    problems, 45–47
  high deductible insurance
    and, 79–80
  increased, for smoking, 102
  Kaiser Family Foundation
    data, 50–51
  medical loss ratios calcula-
    tions, 148
Health Maintenance Organization
  Act, 20
Health savings accounts (HSAs),
  44, 163
*Healthy Competition: What's Hold-
  ing Back Health Care and How to
  Free It* (Tanner), 42
Heartland Institute, 155
Heritage Foundation, 114, 141
HHS. See Department of Health
  and Human Services
High deductible insurance
  CBO data, 81
  diminished benefits, 79–82
  eHealthInsurance.com data,
    80
  Obama's health care proposal,
    81–82
  PPACA and, 91
  premium hikes and, 79–80
  RAND study predictions, 85
Himmelstein, David U., 28
Hispanics, uninsured data, 23

HIV (human immunodeficiency
  virus) infection, 74, 86–87
HMOs (health maintenance
  organizations)
  PPO coverage vs., 50
  subscriber provider selection,
    49–50
Ho, Jessica, 76–78
Holtz-Eakin, Douglas, 162
Hood, James R., 28
House, James, 87
HSAs (health savings accounts),
  44
Hypertension (high blood
  pressure), 60, 85

I

Illegal immigrants
  California and Texas, 93
  PPACA exemption, 92
  uninsurance data, 23, 42
  universal coverage and, 139
Indian Health Program (Native
  Americans), 92
Individual insurance mandate
  alternatives to, 111–113
  centrality to health reform,
    101–103
  constitutionality of, 107–110,
    116–117
  Militia Act of 1792 vs., 114–
    116
  possible compromises, 113
  precedent for, no, 114–117
  precedent for, yes, 101–106
  Proposition C (in Missouri),
    111
  support recommendation,
    97–100
  See also Patient Protection and
    Affordable Care Act

Institute of Medicine (IOM)
  importance of health insurance, 52–57
  mortality rate information, 26
  reports on insurance (2001-2004), 52
  study on insurance-less people, 23, 37, 83–84
Internal Revenue Code mandate, 121–122

J

Jessen, Walter, 65–68
Johns Hopkins Children's Center, 25
Journal of Public Health, 25

K

Kaiser Family Foundation
  employer/self-insured premium data, 50–51
  family of four premium estimates, 146
  health insurance/health study, 69–70
  low income people report, 71
  out of pocket payment observation, 24
  relative risk ratio report, 72
Kaplan, George, 87
Kazzi, Nayla, 31–34
Kingsdale, Jon, 95
Klein, Ezra, 35–36, 40, 83
Klukowski, Ken, 108
Kronick, Richard, 39, 73

L

Landmark: The Inside Story of America's New Health Care Law and What It Means for Us All (Washington Post), 90

Latino, Bradley, 104
Lesley, Bruce, 26
Levy, Helen, 40
Lieberman, Joseph, 35, 40
Los Angeles County, uninsured rates, 56

M

MacGillis, Alec, 90–96
Mahar, Maggie, 69–75, 101–106
Maine, insurance experiment failure, 153
Managed care plans, 49
Massachusetts
  increasing costs, 153–154
  individual mandate experiment, 94–95
  RAND Corporation report, 154
  uninsured rates, 55–56
Mathematica Policy Research, Inc., 58
Matthews, Merrill, 156
McArdle, Megan, 35–41, 83, 85, 86
McClellan, Mark B., 128–130
McWilliams, J. Michael, 85
Medicaid program, 17
  adoption of, 20
  cancer diagnosis, 68
  citizens dumped into, 140–141
  delayed expansion (2014), 124, 125
  eligibility numbers, 42
  FPL eligibility, 63
  guaranteed availability for, 62
  out-of-pocket medical costs, 30
  patient nonacceptance by physicians, 66
  people covered by, 22
  testing for women, 67

Medical bankruptcies
  American Journal of Medicine
    article, 28–29
  IOM study, 23
  Medicaid model recommenda-
    tion, 152
  medical vs. other causes, 30
  reasons for, 18
  US data, 28–29
Medical care
  economics of, 86
  evidence-based improvements,
    129–130
  hi-tech medicine, 73
  Medicare deficiencies, 85–86
  overestimating importance of,
    70–72
  patient vs. government power,
    162–163
Medicare program, 17
  adoption of, 20
  age-related eligibility, 85
  increased medical consump-
    tion, 40
  medical care outcomes, 85–86
  Medicare for all option, 111
  out-of-pocket medical costs,
    30
  people covered by, 22
  prescription drug coverage,
    96, 125
  relation to PPACA, 126
  spending concerns, 36
  2014 expansion, 126
Meltzer, David, 40
Men
  loss of insurance data, 33,
    131–132
  Militia Act (1792), 115–116
  private insurance benefits, 67
  prostatectomy data, 149
Metropolitan Life insurance company, 19

Middle-class families
  HIV/AIDS and autism advo-
    cacy, 74
  increased taxes for, 47
  medical bankruptcies, 28, 30,
    102
Militia Act (of 1792), 104–106,
  114
Missouri, opposition to PPACA,
  146
*Money-Driven Medicine: The Real
  Reason Health Care Costs So
  Much* (Mahar), 69, 101

N

National Academy of Sciences
  (US), 23, 52
National Cancer Database, 65
National Center for Health Statis-
  tics (CDC), 65, 140
National Health and Nutrition
  Examination Survey (1971-
  1987), 37
National Health Interview Survey,
  65, 66
National Institutes of Health, 74
Native Americans
  PPACA exemptions, 92
  uninsured data, 23
New York Times science article, 77
Nix, Kathryn, 139–144

O

Obama, Barack
  broken health insurance
    promise, 144
  CHIP reauthorization, 26
  citizen view of reforms of,
    46–47
  criticism of, 45, 156–157

health care reform speech, 34
See also Patient Protection and Affordable Care Act
"Obamacare." *See* Patient Protection and Affordable Care Act
The Obamacare Disaster: An Appraisal of the Patient Protection and Affordable Care Act (Ferrara), 155
O'Neill, June, 43
Organisation for Economic Cooperation and Development (OECD), 76
"The Original Individual Mandate, Circa 1792" (Latino), 104
Ovation Pharmaceuticals Company, 146

P

Pallarito, Karen, 25–27
Patient-Centered Outcomes Research Institute, 149
Patient Protection and Affordable Care Act (PPACA)
    benefits for uninsured women, 131–135
    cancer care limitations, 145–150
    CBO score for, 160, 162
    Congressional enactment, 20, 124
    Cuccinelli's opposition, 114
    delayed changes (2014), 124, 125
    exemptions from coverage, 92–93
    Ferrara's disagreement with, 156–157
    individual mandate, historical precedent, 101–106

    individual mandate, reasons for supporting, 97–100
"individual responsibility requirement," 119
    meaning for patients, 90–91
    Medicare's relation to, 126
    not choosing coverage, 91–92
    opportunities for improved health care, 128–130
    penalties for not getting coverage, 93–94
    plan information, 90, 124–126
    policy maker considerations, 63–64
    political challenges created by, 95–96
    prescription drug coverage, 124–125
    Rasmussen Reports opinion, 46–47
    Republican Party opposition, 46, 100
    unaffordability of coverage, 92
    uninsured women's benefits, 131–135
Pauly, Mark, 43
Payment for health insurance. *See* Health insurance premiums
Pelosi, Nancy, 155, 161
Peterson, Stephanie, 58–64
Physicians
    adult delayed visits, 55
    community-level, 56
    forced patient changing, 148
    incentives for, 149
    Medicaid patient nonacceptance, 66
    office-based, 66
    as population health champions, 74–75
    reimbursement rate reductions, 141

Physicians for a National Health Program, 145

Pipes, Sally, 156

Politico, 108

PolitiFact.com, 73

Pollack, Harold, 83–88

Poverty level data, 22

PPACA. See Patient Protection and Affordable Care Act

PPOs (preferred provider organizations)
co-payments/out-of-pocket costs, 50–51
growth of, vs. HMOs, 49–50

Preexisting conditions, 18–19

Premature deaths, 55, 58–59, 61–62, 69, 73, 103

Preston, Samuel, 76–78

Preventive services for children and adults, 59

Preventive Services Task Force (US), 63–64

Private insurance
Medicaid-insured vs., 67–68
Obamacare Medicare vs., 159
out-of-pocket medical costs, 30
physician patient acceptance, 66
"progressives" defense of, 111
public insurance vs., 112
purchaser profile, 17–18
single-payer system recommendation, 29
universal access and, 86
women's testing, 67
See also Employer-based health insurance

Proposition C (in Missouri), 111

Prudential insurance company, 19

Q

Quality issues and the Patient Protection and Affordable Care Act, 128–129

R

RAND Health Insurance Experiment (HIE), 39–40, 70–71, 84–85

Rasmussen Reports
cost vs. coverage problem, 45
views of Obama's reforms, 46–47

Reagan, Ronald, 99, 155

"The Real Costs and Consequences of the New Health Care Law" (Tanner), 101

Reason magazine, 76

Recession (US)
downward coverage spiral, 53–54
employer-based losses, 33
industries influenced by, 32–33
patients stopping drug use from, 147
pre-recession data, 32
uninsured increases from, 31–34

Reid, Harry, 161

Republican Party
deflection of uninsurance issue, 36
health care plan opposition, 46, 100
Romney universal coverage plan, 95, 100

Restoring the Lost Constitution: The Presumption of Liberty, 118–122

Romney, Mitt
FOX News interview, 100
universal coverage plan, 95,
100
See also Massachusetts
Rustgi, Sheila, 131–135

S

Scandlen, Greg, 156
SCHIP (State Children's Health
Insurance Program), 20
Schoeni, Robert, 87
Schroeder, SA, 73, 74–75
Sebelius, Kathleen, 79
Shattuck Lecture (Schroeder,
2007), 73–74
Shaw, Julia, 114–117
Single-payer health care system.
See Universal health coverage
Smoking
cessation programs, 66–67
deaths related to, 86
increased premiums, 102
Social Security Institute, 15555
Sonzinsky v. U.S. (1937), 121
Spending (economics)
actions for reducing, 57
co-payments/out-of-pocket
costs, 50–51, 79
controlling growth of, 87–88
Medicare spending, 36
Stanford University, 43
State-based insurance market-
places, 90–91
State Children's Health Insurance
Program (SCHIP), 20, 22, 42, 62
enrollment barriers, 26
Johns Hopkins study, 26–27
Stroke victims, 59
Suderman, Peter, 151–154

Supreme Court
Bailey v. Drexel Furniture Co.,
120
individual mandate constitutionality, no, 118–122
individual mandate constitutionality, yes, 107–110
interstate commerce regulations, 107
Klukowski's argument, 108
Sonzinsky v. U.S., 121
tax rules and regulations, 109
U.S. v. Kahriger, 121

T

Tanner, Michael, 23, 42–44, 101,
103–104
Taxes
employer/government deductions, 18–19
health savings accounts, 44
individual mandate tax, 112
Internal Revenue Code mandate, 121–122
Social Security taxes, 109
tobacco use, 86
Tennessee, health insurance failure, 141, 151–153
Texas
immigrant hospital care, 93
uninsured rates, 55–56
Tierney, John, 77
Tobacco. *See* Smoking
Turner, Grace-Marie, 156

U

Underinsured citizens, 30
Uninsured citizens
at-risk populations, 58, 59
cancer death risks, 65–68

cost vs. lack of coverage,
45–47
death of uninsured children,
25–27
influence of recession, 31–34
IOM data/studies, 23–24, 37
Kaiser Family Foundation
data, 24
likelihood of death vs. insured, 35–41
Los Angeles County rates, 56
low US life expectancy, 76–78
Massachusetts/Texas rates,
55–56
men vs. women, 33–34
poor health outcomes, 58–60
profile, 22–23, 38
research problems, 36–39
rising number estimates,
32–33
risks to communities, 55–57
specific disease death risks,
71–72
wealthy young people as,
42–44
United States
bankruptcy prediction, 161–
162
declining coverage spiral,
53–54
Great Depression, 18
health strategy, 73–74
low life expectancy, 76–78
Medicare/Medicaid adoption,
20
Militia Act (of 1792), 114–116
minority communities, 85
national health care debate, 36
Obamacare as disaster, 155–
163
patient vs. government power,
162–163

Universal health coverage
consumer activism for, 28
Democrat vs. Republican feel-
ings, 46–47
as individual mandate alterna-
tive, 111
as one tool for health im-
provement, 83–88
Rasmussen Reports findings,
45–46
University of California, San Di-
ego, 39
University of Chicago, 40, 83
University of Michigan, 40
University of Pennsylvania, 43,
76–77
*The Untold Story of America's
Health Care Crisis-and the People
Who Pay the Price* (Cohn), 97
Urban Institute, 36–37, 38
U.S. v. Kahriger (1953), 121
US Federal Reserve, 154
US National Academy of Sciences,
23, 52
US Preventive Services Task Force,
63–64

V

Veterans Affair (VA) insurance, 30

W

Walker, Jon, 111–113
Washington, George, 104–106
Washington Post, 90
White House Office of Policy Development, 155
Women
benefits of PPACA, 131–135
cigarette consumption data,
77

consequences of no insurance, 55

employer coverage inequalities, 33

preventive services requirements, 63–64

private insurance benefits, 67

World War II, 19

Y

Yglesias, Matthew, 35